THE ADOLESCENT RELAPSE PREVENTION PLANNER

JENNIFER BRUHA, Ph.D.

TURNING
STONE
PRESS

First published in 2012 by Turning Stone Press, an imprint of Red Wheel/Weiser, LLC
With offices at:
665 Third Street, Suite 400
San Francisco, CA 94107
www.redwheelweiser.com

ISBN (paperback): 978-1-61852-025-8
ISBN (hardcover): 978-1-61852-024-1

Cover design by Jim Warner
Interior design by Frame25 Productions

Printed in the United States of America
IBT
10 9 8 7 6 5 4 3 2 1

In dedication to

my parents, Don and Janis Bruha,
my grandfather, James Bruha,
and adolescents everywhere.

Contents

An Introduction for Professionals

Substance abuse is an ever-increasing problem, particularly among adolescents, who are exposed at younger ages to newer and stronger drugs with higher addictive potential and greater availability. Prescription drug use has exploded as prescriptions are more widely marketed to the public and are made available over the Internet. "Pharm" parties are increasingly popular among adolescents, with medications acquired via home medicine cabinets. Illicit drug use continues to be on the rise, and drugs like meth, coke, and ecstasy are now associated with greater long-term health problems. Marijuana, spice, and other "natural" drugs, whether legal or illegal, are still popular, as they are relatively cheap compared to other drugs, and are more socially acceptable. Moreover, over-the-counter drugs like cough and cold medications and cough syrups have become an inexpensive and easy way to get high.

Consequently, this leaves more adolescents feeling unmotivated and unwilling to attend school, complete homework, and fulfill responsibilities, opening the gateway for drug experimentation, behavioral problems, and dropping out of school.

In this high-stress world, where temptations are everywhere, the economy is in crisis, crime and violence are on the rise, and families are increasingly defined by dysfunction and/or single-parent households, adolescents search for that quick fix to escape from reality. Unfortunately for many, that desire for a quick fix leads to substance abuse and even addiction, which impacts puberty and adolescent development physically, psychologically, and emotionally. This presents unique challenges in treatment and recovery. Adolescent treatment programs and specialists are grossly underfunded and unavailable; leading to the importance of relapse prevention planning that takes into consideration the special circumstances of adolescence.

This workbook addresses the challenges adolescents face in their recovery, regardless of where they fit in the stages of change process. This workbook is intended for use by professionals treating adolescents with substance abuse problems, by treatment programs, and even by adolescents themselves. This may be used as a curriculum or guide for groups that focus on problem identification, drug education, and relapse prevention, or as an adjunct to day treatment, outpatient, inpatient, and residential programs.

This workbook contains eight chapters with exercises for individuals that can be reproduced. There are also discussion topics and exercises for groups at the end of each section that are meant to be interesting, thought-provoking, psycho-educational, and even fun, making treatment and the recovery process more manageable and achievable.

1

Defining and Identifying the Problem

Weighing the Advantages and Disadvantages of Using

One of the first steps in recovery from substance abuse and addiction is identifying the advantages and disadvantages of continued use and to living a clean and sober lifestyle. Or you can look at it in a different way, listing the reasons to use and not to use substances. In the table below, identify the advantages and disadvantages of using substances, followed by the advantages and disadvantages of getting and staying clean.

ADVANTAGES OF USING (reasons to use)	DISADVANTAGES OF USING (reasons not to use)
Calming Relaxing Avoiding Anger _____ _____ _____	Developing Health Problems Getting Arrested Dying _____ _____ _____
ADVANTAGES OF LIVING A CLEAN AND SOBER LIFESTYLE (abstinence)	DISADVANTAGES OF LIVING A CLEAN AND SOBER LIFESTYLE
Being Healthy Having No Legal Problems Getting Off Probation _____ _____ _____	Going Through Withdrawal Having to Avoid Certain Friends Avoiding Parties _____ _____ _____

Group Discussion Topics for Weighing the Advantages and Disadvantages of Using

GROUP DISCUSSION

One reason to use is the "quick fix" a drug gives us. But, taking it one step further, what is it that we are trying to "fix?" Do we use merely to get high and feel good; or is there something underneath that drives the use, like poor self-esteem? Is the "quick fix" about stress reduction or avoidance of something? Discuss what group members are looking for in a "quick fix" and possible alternatives to drugs.

GROUP DISCUSSION

Sometimes substances seem to make us more social and fun, as they reduce our self-consciousness thus increasing sociability. This is often the case with ecstasy or alcohol. Because of increased sociability, users often have greater difficulty giving up the substance(s). Discuss this as a group.

GROUP DISCUSSION

As a group, compare the advantages and disadvantages of using. Which category has more reasons listed? Are the advantages of using the same or similar to the disadvantages of living clean and sober? Are the disadvantages of using the same or similar to the advantages of living clean and sober? What can be concluded from this? Does this strengthen or reduce the overall desire to use substances?

GROUP DISCUSSION

If "substances" are replaced with one particular drug (e.g., cigarettes, alcohol, meth), do any of the advantages or disadvantages change? What if these substances are replaced with addictive behaviors (e.g., gambling, eating, cutting, shopping)? Discuss.

Substance Abuse vs. Addiction

Definition of a Drug

A drug may be defined as anything that changes the chemical make-up of the brain or body. This includes illicit drugs (e.g., heroin, meth, coke), alcohol, prescription drugs (e.g., painkillers, sedatives, tranquilizers, amphetamines), over-the-counter medications, inhalants, and nicotine.

However, compulsive behaviors can also change the chemical make-up of the brain and lead to addiction (e.g., gambling, eating, shopping); hence, the terms "substance use" and "substance abuse" are more accurate and are preferred over "drug use" and "drug abuse."

Treatment may differ somewhat depending on whether someone has a substance abuse problem or an addiction. Therefore, one of the first steps in recovery is to understand the difference between them.

Substance Abuse

Substance abuse may be defined in several ways: repeatedly taking too much of a given substance (e.g., binge drinking); taking a substance for a purpose other than that for which it is intended (e.g., trying to get high on prescription medications); using illegal substances (e.g., snorting cocaine, smoking marijuana); and overdosing. Substance abuse may become a pattern or habit. There may be recurrent use in hazardous situations or negative effects resulting in legal, financial, educational, or social problems as well (APA, 2000).

EXERCISE

Ask yourself the following questions:

1. Have I repeatedly used a substance(s) in excess in the past year? If so, what substance(s) did I take and how much?

   _____

   _____

   _____

2. Have I repeatedly used a substance(s) for a purpose other than that for which it is intended or prescribed? (Example: taking cough and cold medications or cough syrup to get high.) If so, what?

   _____

   _____

   _____

3. Has my substance use resulted in problems at home, work, or school? If so, what are those problems?

_____

_____

_____

4. Has my substance use resulted in interpersonal problems (with family members, friends, significant others, partners)? If so, with whom?

_____

_____

_____

5. Has my substance use resulted in legal problems (e.g., probation, juvenile hall)?

_____

_____

_____

6. Have I repeatedly used substances in hazardous situations (e.g., drinking and driving), and if so, what are those situations?

_____

_____

_____

Addiction

Addiction, or substance dependence, is substance abuse taken to the extreme, leading to changes in the chemical make-up of the brain and body. Addiction is largely characterized by the presence of tolerance, withdrawal symptoms, and continued use despite its negative effects in other areas of life (work, school, family, social life) (APA, 2000). Tolerance is defined as needing greater amounts of a given substance to get the same effect—for example, needing a six-pack of beer to get tipsy when, at first, it was only one or two beers. Withdrawal symptoms occur when the drugs wear off or when the drugs aren't used, which increases the desire to use again to avoid or stop the symptoms—examples include nausea, vomiting, diarrhea, anxiety, and fever. Withdrawal symptoms are typically the reverse of the drugs' effects as the body tries to regain balance (homeostasis).

Answer the following questions, based on the answers you gave to the questions in the previous section on substance abuse.

1. What substances have I abused in the past twelve months? Check all that apply.

_____Alcohol	_____Amphetamines
_____Caffeine	_____Codeine
_____Coke/crack	_____Cold and cough medications
_____Ecstasy/MDMA	_____GHB or Rohypnol
_____Heroin	_____Inhalants
_____Ketamine	_____LSD
_____Marijuana	_____Methadone
_____Methamphetamine/speed	_____Mushrooms/psilocybin
_____Morphine	_____Nicotine/tobacco
_____Opium	_____PCP
_____Peyote	_____Prescription painkillers
_____Prescription stimulants	_____Salvia
_____Spice	_____Whippets

2. Addictions can also include behaviors like eating (which can lead to eating disorders and/or obesity), compulsive behaviors, and self-harm behaviors. These are also known as process addictions. Have I engaged in any of these behaviors? Check all that apply.

_____Eating, fasting, or dieting

_____Exercising to excess (several hours per day every day)

_____Gambling

_____Having sex, watching pornography or Internet porn, engaging in sexual acts (multiple times per day every day)

_____Self-harming (cutting, burning, beating self)

_____Shopping

3. What substances have I taken in increasingly larger amounts to get the same effect? Check all that apply.

_____Alcohol	_____Amphetamines
_____Caffeine	_____Codeine
_____Coke/crack	_____Cold and cough medications
_____Ecstasy/MDMA	_____GHB or rohypnol
_____Heroin	_____Inhalants
_____Ketamine	_____LSD
_____Marijuana	_____Methadone
_____Methamphetamine/speed	_____Mushrooms/psilocybin
_____Morphine	_____Nicotine/tobacco
_____Opium	_____PCP
_____Peyote	_____Prescription painkillers

_____Prescription stimulants   _____Salvia

_____Spice   _____Whippets

4. Have I experienced withdrawal symptoms? Check all that apply.

_____Anxiety, nervousness	_____Fever, chills, cold sweats
_____Nausea, vomiting, diarrhea	_____Increase/decrease in heart rate
_____Changes in blood pressure	_____Shakiness, tremors
_____Fatigue, exhaustion	_____Insomnia
_____Changes in eating	_____Severe aches and pains
_____Headaches	_____Muscle cramps
_____Motor problems	_____Lack of coordination
_____Hallucinations	_____Delusions
_____Paranoia	_____Psychosis
_____Seizures	_____Cravings

5. What are the negative effects of my substance abuse on my life? Check all that apply.

AT HOME	AT SCHOOL
_____Verbal conflict	_____Truancy
_____Physical conflict	_____Chronic tardiness
_____Loss of trust	_____Bad grades or drop in grades
_____Ran away once	_____Behind in school credits
_____Ran away frequently	_____Suspensions
_____Loss of family	_____Expulsions
_____Homelessness	_____Dropped out of school

AT WORK	LEGAL PROBLEMS
_____Chronic tardiness	_____Citations
_____Frequent absences	_____Drug-related charges
_____Write-ups	_____Drug-related convictions
_____Suspensions	_____DUIs, DWIs
_____Job loss	_____Fines, restitution
_____Unemployment	_____Juvenile hall/jail
	_____House arrest
	_____Community service
	_____Probation/parole
	_____Civil suits

_____Loss of friends

_____Loss of social status

_____Gang affiliation/involvement

Group Exercises and Discussion Topics for Substance Abuse vs. Addiction

GROUP EXERCISE

Part of substance abuse and especially addiction is a preoccupation with thoughts of use. Have the group identify all the different thoughts they experience during the day regarding their substance use. For example, "When can I smoke?" "When can I drink?" "How am I going to get to the dealer?" "Where am I going to stash it?" "Where am I going to get the money?" Have a group member write down all these thoughts on a board. Then discuss how this affects daily life and substance use.

GROUP DISCUSSION

Often, we don't realize how much, how often, or how many substances we are abusing until we really think about it or see it in writing. We enter treatment for meth addiction, for example, and in the treatment process realize we have also been abusing other substances like alcohol, marijuana, or nicotine. This can be difficult to deal with. Have the group discuss how their substance abuse has increased or worsened and what factors led up to it. Some group members may realize they are actually addicted to other substances when tolerance and withdrawal are factored in. What do group members think? How can they cope with this?

GROUP DISCUSSION

Addiction is substance abuse taken to the extreme, so substance abuse may be considered a prerequisite for developing substance dependence. Is it possible for an addict not to have a substance abuse problem? What does the group think?

GROUP DISCUSSION

Often in recovery, when we abstain from using our drug(s) of choice, we take up "bad habits" (e.g., smoking cigarettes, overeating, self-harming). We convince ourselves the "bad habits" are less harmful—an excuse we use to justify their continued use. These substances and behaviors can become repetitive and frequent, or addictive in and of themselves. Thus, we are really just replacing one substance with another substance or behavior. Have the group discuss this aspect of recovery. Can any of them relate? Do any of the group members have these "bad habits," and are their justifications valid? How does this affect recovery from the primary drug(s) of choice?

GROUP EXERCISE: WORD SEARCH

This exercise can be done individually or groups can compete to see which one finds all the words first.

Directions:
Find the words and phrases that describe addiction in the puzzle. They may be backward, forward, up, or down.

WORDS TO FIND:
Abuse, Dependence, Disease, Impulsiveness, Chemistry, Tolerance, Isolation, Out of Control, Numb the Feelings

```
N  U  M  B  T  H  E  F  E  E  L  I  N  G  S  C
O  Y  D  E  L  P  M  I  C  H  O  R  I  W  O  U
I  E  S  A  E  S  I  D  A  I  H  T  S  I  N  N
T  A  N  S  C  T  N  E  C  N  A  R  E  L  O  T
A  B  O  U  I  S  O  P  Y  S  N  M  I  S  B  W
L  R  N  D  J  R  T  E  C  H  A  E  S  T  A  E
O  H  T  A  E  T  A  N  Y  I  E  S  L  I  E  N
S  E  A  T  P  E  M  D  O  S  T  U  I  L  Y  M
I  A  S  R  K  S  O  E  W  I  S  B  P  I  N  T
H  U  I  M  I  R  Y  N  E  A  G  A  I  O  U  L
L  K  T  I  B  N  S  C  H  E  M  I  S  T  R  Y
P  E  N  T  A  L  H  E  O  L  C  H  I  X  I  W
T  S  A  O  T  M  I  Q  I  R  Y  O  U  S  D  N
C  B  E  A  N  H  T  L  O  U  S  M  T  N  A  E
O  U  T  O  F  C  O  N  T  R  O  L  E  A  N  V
F  O  I  Y  Y  T  E  A  N  L  R  S  U  P  H  W
U  S  S  E  N  E  V  I  S  L  U  P  M  I  E  S
```

```
N U M B T H E F E E L I N G S C
O Y D E L P M I C H O R I W O U
I E S A E S I D A I H T S I N N
T A N S C T N E C N A R E L O T
A B O U I S O P Y S N M I S B W
L R N D J R T E C H A E S T A E
O H T A E T A N Y I E S L I E N
S E A T P E M D O S T U I L Y M
I A S R K S O E W I S B P I N T
H U I M I R Y N E A G A I O U L
L K T I B N S C H E M I S T R Y
P E N T A L H E O L C H I X I W
T S A O T M I Q I R Y O U S D N
C B E A N H T L O U S M T N A E
O U T O F C O N T R O L E A N V
F O I Y Y T E A N L R S U P H W
U S S E N E V I S L U P M I E S
```

How Others Perceive My Use

Sometimes we need another person(s) whom we trust to "give us the honest truth" about our use when we can't be objective about it. Feedback from a family member, friend, or confidant may help us recognize that we have a problem with substances, regardless of whether it is substance abuse or addiction.

EXERCISE

Have a conversation about your substance use with a parent, family member, and two peers. Ask them to answer the following questions, and then get their signatures. Have them write their answers.

Parent:

1. Do you think I have a problem with substances? If so, what makes you think I have a problem?

   _____
   _____
   _____

2. When did you first notice I had a problem with substances?

   _____
   _____
   _____

3. How have my attitude and behaviors changed since I began using?

   _____
   _____
   _____

Signature:_____

Family Member:

1. Do you think I have a problem with substances? If so, what makes you think I have a problem?

   _____
   _____
   _____

2. When did you first notice I had a problem with substances?

_____

_____

_____

3. How have my attitude and behaviors changed since I began using?

_____

_____

_____

Signature:_____

Peer 1:
1. Do you think I have a problem with substances? If so, what makes you think I have a problem?

_____

_____

_____

2. When did you first notice I had a problem with substances?

_____

_____

_____

3. How have my attitude and behaviors changed since I began using?

_____

_____

_____

Signature:_____

Peer 2:

1. Do you think I have a problem with substances? If so, what makes you think I have a problem?

   _____

   _____

   _____

2. When did you first notice I had a problem with substances?

   _____

   _____

   _____

3. How have my attitude and behaviors changed since I began using?

   _____

   _____

   _____

Signature:_____

EXERCISE

Answer the following questions based on the responses to the exercise above:

1. How did it make you feel to hear/read the responses from your parent, family member, and peers?

   _____

   _____

   _____

2. Do any of their responses surprise you?

   _____

   _____

   _____

3. Do you agree or disagree with their responses?

_____

_____

_____

4. Based on their responses and what you know about your substance use, do you think you have a problem with substances? Why or why not?

_____

_____

_____

Group Discussion Topics for How Others Perceive My Use

GROUP DISCUSSION

Have group members share what it was like to have conversations about their substance use. Was anyone surprised at the feedback they received? What feelings came up? How did they work through or cope with the feedback and resulting emotions? Was anyone's feedback weighed more heavily (mattered more) than others? Why? What did group members learn from this exercise?

GROUP DISCUSSION

Looking at Question #2 (When did you first notice I had a problem with substances?), have group members discuss the various responses they received. Were there any patterns in responses? Were answers varied or similar? Did substance abuse become evident around specific times, incidents, traumas, or ages? Did group members learn anything about their own use and how others perceive it?

GROUP DISCUSSION

What changes in attitude and behaviors were identified by family members (in Question #3)? Discuss.

GROUP DISCUSSION

This is a good exercise in challenging denial. Did some in the group come to the realization of having a substance abuse problem that, up until now, they have denied? Or, did some conclude that they are beyond substance abuse and are addicted to one or more substances? Process thoughts and feelings that came up around this breakthrough of denial.

If I Continue to Abuse Substances . . .

Finish the following statements by checking all that apply:

1. *If I continue to abuse substances and/or relapse, I could:*
   - ☐ physically harm my body
   - ☐ emotionally/mentally harm myself
   - ☐ develop a serious physical condition (e.g., heart attack, stroke)
   - ☐ develop a serious psychological condition (e.g., brain damage, depression)
   - ☐ be hospitalized
   - ☐ overdose
   - ☐ experiment with harder/worse drugs
   - ☐ start using needles
   - ☐ become suicidal and/or attempt suicide
   - ☐ die

2. *If I continue to abuse substances and/or relapse, I could:*
   - ☐ lose my family's trust
   - ☐ hurt my family and friends
   - ☐ lie to my family and friends
   - ☐ steal from my family and friends
   - ☐ get thrown out of my house/be homeless

3. *If I continue to abuse substances and/or relapse, I could:*
   - ☐ be arrested
   - ☐ go to juvenile hall
   - ☐ go to jail
   - ☐ violate probation
   - ☐ end up on probation
   - ☐ be mandated to treatment
   - ☐ be institutionalized

4. *If I continue to abuse substances and/or relapse, I could:*

    ☐ skip classes/school

    ☐ get poor grades

    ☐ flunk out

    ☐ be suspended

    ☐ be expelled from school

    ☐ end up in continuation school

    ☐ drop out

    ☐ prevent myself from graduating or attaining a GED

    ☐ lose out on college and/or scholarships

5. *If I continue to abuse substances and/or relapse, I could:*

    ☐ lose my job

    ☐ lose opportunities for other jobs

6. *If I continue to abuse substances and/or relapse, I could:*

_____

7. *What would a relapse look like for me? I would most likely use/abuse:*

_____

EXERCISE: TOMBSTONE AND OBITUARY

One unfortunate consequence of continued use is death, which can result from an overdose, using too many substances together, driving under the influence, or engaging in other risky behaviors while intoxicated. On the following pages, you can explore how you want to be remembered if you pass away today from substance-related causes. First, design your tombstone. Then, write your obituary. Make sure to include the following: the years you were born and died; who survives you (e.g., parents, siblings, grandparents, etc.); and how you want to be remembered. Then share what you wrote with a counselor and/or in a group.

TOMBSTONE

The Adolescent Relapse Prevention Planner

OBITUARY

Group Exercises and Discussion Topics for *If I Continue to Abuse Substances*

GROUP DISCUSSION

Have group members share their obituaries with the group. What would be written about them if they died today? Explore the feelings and thoughts that came up while doing the exercise. Then explore what they think their families' and friends' reactions would be in response to their deaths.

GROUP EXERCISE

Have group members write a second obituary written after their death at age sixty-five. How would they want to be remembered? Did they have a spouse, children, or grandchildren? What were their goals and dreams, and were they accomplished? What were their jobs or chosen professions? Were they clean?

GROUP DISCUSSION

This discussion follows the group exercise above. Have group members share their second obituary. Discuss how their lives would be different dying at age sixty-five, as opposed to now. Would they be clean and sober? What role does treatment or time play in changing the course of their lives? Is the second obituary more hopeful and motivating? Discuss as a group.

Consequences of Substance Use

Part of recovery involves recognizing and acknowledging the effects of substance abuse on all aspects of life and the people in it.

EXERCISE

Answer the following questions:

1. Has my substance abuse/addiction contributed to or directly caused the following problems? Check all that apply.

_____ Overdose

_____ Sleep problems

_____ Loss of energy

_____ Malnutrition

_____ Weight loss, weight gain

_____ Vitamin deficiency

_____ Breathing problems, asthma

_____ Emphysema

_____ Chronic lung disease

_____ Chronic bronchitis

_____ Pneumonia

_____ Heart attack

_____ Heart problems

_____ Tooth loss, broken teeth

_____ Meth mouth

_____ Chronic nose bleeds

_____ Anxiety, nervousness, tremors

_____ Headaches

_____ Frequent or chronic pain

_____ Infections, blood disease

_____ Track marks

_____ Collapsed veins

_____ Hepatitis

_____ HIV, AIDS

_____ Suppressed immune system

_____ Gastrointestinal problems

_____ Kidney problems

_____ Hormonal irregularities

_____ Delayed puberty

_____ STDs (from unprotected sex)

_____ Pregnancy

_____ Other

2. Has my substance abuse/addiction contributed to or directly caused the following psychological and/or emotional problems? Check all that apply.

_____ Depression

_____ Extreme mood swings

_____ Anxiety

_____ Memory loss/problems

_____ Cognitive impairments (in decision-making, problem-solving, comprehension)

_____ Problems with concentration and/or inattention)

_____ Speech problems

_____ Blackouts or lapse of consciousness

_____ Hallucinations

_____ Delusions

_____ Brain damage

_____ Paranoia

_____ Psychosis

_____ Coma

_____ Stroke

_____ Other

3. Has my substance abuse/addiction contributed to the following problems at home? Check all that apply.

_____ Conflict with family members   _____ Disregard for house rules

_____ Arguments   _____ Sibling substance use

_____ Disrespect toward family members   _____ Theft (e.g., stealing money, items)

_____ Dishonesty   _____ Punishment (e.g., being grounded)

_____ Loss of trust   _____ Loss of privileges

_____ Manipulation (of family members)

_____ Aggression/violence

4. Has my substance abuse/addiction contributed to the following problems at school? Check all that apply.

_____ Loss of interest in school   _____ Loss of motivation

_____ Chronic tardiness   _____ Decline in grades, flunking out

_____ Truancy   _____ Lower GPA

_____ Loss of attention, focus,   _____ Behind in school credits
      or concentration   _____ Suspensions

_____ Problems with teachers   _____ Expulsions

_____ Decreased or stopped   _____ Dropping out of school
      participation in sports and   _____ Transferring schools
      other after-school activities

5. Has my substance abuse/addiction contributed to the following problems at work? Check all that apply.

_____ Chronic tardiness   _____ Demotions

_____ Excessive absences   _____ Job loss

_____ Excessive errors   _____ Unemployment

_____ Write-ups

6. Has my substance abuse/addiction contributed to the following illegal activities and/or legal problems? Check all that apply.

_____ Drug citations   _____ Assault and/or battery

_____ Drug-related charges   _____ Attempted murder

_____ Drug-related convictions   _____ Manslaughter

_____ DUIs/DWIs   _____ Time spent in juvenile hall, jail

_____ Possession   _____ Community service

_____ Selling drugs   _____ Fines, restitution

_____ Manufacturing drugs   _____ On probation, parole

_____ Prostitution   _____ House arrest

_____	Theft, robbery, burglary, grand theft auto	_____	Probation violations
_____	Vandalism, trespass	_____	Drug court
_____	Weapons charges	_____	Lawsuits, civil suits

7. Has my substance abuse/addiction contributed to the following financial problems for myself and/or my parents? Check all that apply.

_____	Debt (borrowed money)	_____	Loss of income
_____	Debt (credit cards)	_____	Increased insurance rates
_____	Late payments		

8. Has my substance abuse/addiction contributed to the following problems in my social life or social activities? Check all that apply.

_____	Conflict with friends	_____	Greater involvement in negative relationships with people who use
_____	Loss of friendships		
_____	Problems with significant others (e.g., boyfriend, girlfriend, partner)	_____	Loss of roles (e.g., athlete, mentor, coach, artist, scout)

9. Has my substance abuse/addiction contributed to the following spiritual/religious problems? Check all that apply.

_____	Loss of spiritual beliefs	_____	Reduction in spiritual practices
_____	Loss of spiritual identity		

Group Exercises and Discussion Topics for Consequences of Substance Use

GROUP DISCUSSION

Discuss which physical, emotional, and psychological problems/symptoms were identified by group members, and whether they increase or decrease the desire to use. For example, some drugs can cause long-term depression, which, in turn, can fuel continued drug use in an effort to avoid feeling depressed. (But in reality, it only makes the depression worse!) Discuss how these physical, emotional, and psychological problems/symptoms have affected the lives of group members, their families, and, expanding outward, the wider community.

GROUP DISCUSSION

The primary job of an adolescent is to achieve a high school diploma (or GED), but substance abuse can interfere with that pursuit. Discuss how substance use has affected school. Discuss how individuals can "get back on track" academically as they begin the recovery process.

GROUP DISCUSSION

Many adolescents have a rather egocentric view of substance abuse, thinking it only affects them. Discuss how substance abuse is really a family problem. Identify how drug use and drug-related behaviors have affected the families of group members. Discuss how their families have been affected in the following ways:

- Physically (e.g., physical altercations)

- Financially (e.g., accidents, treatment costs, insurance increases)

- Emotionally (e.g., loss of trust, problems with honesty or dependability, communication problems)

GROUP EXERCISE AND DISCUSSION: MOVIE

Watch the movie *Walk the Line* (2005), which depicts the progression of Johnny Cash's substance abuse and his cycle of use. Discuss the following:

- How were substance abuse and addiction depicted in the movie? Was Cash an addict? What were his drugs of choice?

- What events or circumstances in his life may have contributed to his drug use? Can group members relate to these circumstances, or "causes"?

- What were the effects of his drug use? How did drugs affect his career, family, financial situation, and health?

A Letter to my Drug of Choice: Understanding Your Relationship with Your Drug(s) of Choice

The relationship between addicts (possibly you) and their (your) drug(s) of choice—whether it be alcohol, cocaine, nicotine, heroin, or a compulsive behavior like gambling or binge eating—is similar to a relationship between two people. The drug(s) of choice may take on multiple roles with multiple levels of meaning.

The drug(s) of choice can be an addict's best friend in that it is reliable and dependable, and it will never be abusive or mean, as humans may be at times. Addicts love their drug(s) of choice and, over time, begin to believe they cannot live or function normally without it. At first, it is an escape from uncomfortable feelings or situations. It seems to take away the pain, and so the addict turns to it again and again. It can eventually take the place of people.

At the same time, the drug(s) of choice is the addict's worst enemy, capable of destroying him or her with each drink, hit, or puff. Physically, psychologically, and emotionally, it breaks down the body and mind. Addicts think they control the drug but, in reality, the drug(s) of choice controls them; when they try to live without it, withdrawal symptoms appear, making it even more difficult to say no. The drug becomes the reason to live and die.

EXERCISE

In the space provided *(see page 24)* write a letter to your drug(s) of choice, exploring the relationship between you and the drug(s). First, thank the drug(s) for the ways in which it seemed to "help you" (i.e., it was an escape from pain, it made you more social, it was fun) and how it was your best friend at times. Then, tell the drug(s) why you no longer need it and how it has hurt you (i.e., it put you in dangerous situations, led to overdose, led you to the hospital, or to jail). Tell the drug(s) how it is you are recovering (i.e., I'm learning to trust people, I'm sharing painful secrets, making new friends, learning how to cope with my feelings). Keep this letter and refer back to it and/or share it with someone who is also in recovery or with someone who is helping you.

Dear,

Letter to my Drug of Choice

The Adolescent Relapse Prevention Planner

Group Exercises and Discussion Topics for A Letter to My Drug of Choice

GROUP EXERCISE

Give everyone the option of reading their letter out loud. (You may want to reward those who read their letters out loud with some gum or candy, since this can be difficult to do.) Afterward, discuss what feelings came up during this exercise. Allow for feedback.

GROUP DISCUSSION

Substance abuse, and especially addiction, is similar to a relationship between two people in that the substance of choice can be both your best friend and your worst enemy. The substance can be your best friend in that it won't be mean to you, reject you, or leave you, as a person may do. It makes you feel good and takes the pain away (although only temporarily). But, it also slowly consumes you—mentally, emotionally, physically, financially—and eventually may kill you. You *love* it, and you *hate* it, whatever *it* is. Discuss the idea of addiction being like a relationship and your substance of choice (whether it be a drug like cocaine or a behavior like eating or gambling) being your best friend and your enemy. What comes up for group members and how does this relationship affect (or complicate) the process of recovery?

2

Learning About Substances

Stimulants

What drugs are classified as stimulants, and how do they affect the body and brain? Common stimulants include:

- Cocaine

- Crack

- Methamphetamine (crank, speed, ice)

- Amphetamines (e.g., diet pills)

- Ephedrine, pseudoephedrine

- Prescription stimulants (e.g., Ritalin, Adderall)

- Nicotine

- Chewing tobacco

- Caffeine

- Energy drinks

- Ecstasy/MDMA (may also be classified as a psychedelic)

Stimulants generally excite and energize the body and brain. Some stimulants (e.g., coke, crack, crank) cause the release of excess dopamine (a chemical in the brain) and prevent its re-uptake in between neurons (nerve cells). This excites the brain and body, activates the reward-pleasure center, and causes euphoria (the *high*) (NIDA, 2011a; NIDA, 2011b). Following the high, there is a period of *coming down*, as excess dopamine leads to its eventual depletion. This may cause depressed mood, loss of pleasure, fatigue, and sleepiness. The brain will eventually try to return to a level of homeostasis (balance), in which its chemicals (e.g., dopamine, serotonin, adrenalin, etc.) are more equalized, leading to more optimal functioning.

Some drugs are faster-acting, versus slower-acting, depending in part on the drug itself and on the route of administration. Snorting coke or smoking crack, for example, are faster-acting because the body absorbs more of the drug. Users achieve the high faster but sustain it for a shorter period of time—which, in turn, leads to a faster-acting low. The high and low are also steeper. However, users will never achieve the same high as the first time, regardless of the extent of use. In contrast, other drugs like ecstasy (in pill form) taken orally have a slower-acting but longer-lasting high, followed by a longer-lasting low.

While all stimulants initially excite the body, research shows that different stimulants are associated with different short-term and long-term effects. Common physical short-term effects include increased heart rate, pulse, and blood pressure; tachycardia and arrhythmia; restlessness and/or insomnia; anxiety or nervousness; and loss of appetite leading to weight loss. Some stimulants—cocaine, amphetamines, and most notably, methamphetamine—can cause formication, a type of tactile hallucination in which users experience the sensation of bugs crawling on their skin and repeatedly scratch, leaving sores and causing infections (Litt, 2009). This, coupled with increased acne, contribute to premature aging among meth addicts. Another side-effect of methamphetamine abuse is meth mouth, in which the meth wears away tooth enamel, leading to rotted and/or broken teeth, gum disease, and eventual tooth loss. This may be painful and very expensive to treat.

Another increasingly used, but potentially harmful, stimulant is ecstasy, or MDMA (3,4-methylenedioxymethamphetamine), which may also be classified as a psychedelic. Ecstasy has been shown to cause brain damage, particularly to the memory and learning centers of the brain, leading to problems with verbal memory, visual memory, and long-term memory even after a single use (JAMA, 2007; RSNA, 2006). Ecstasy damages neurons that transport and house serotonin, a chemical involved in mood, learning, and memory, leading to cognitive deficits and memory problems (JAMA, 2007; RSNA, 2006).

The second most commonly abused stimulant, after caffeine, is nicotine, which has been associated with increased rates of cancers of the lungs, mouth, throat, and esophagus, as well as chronic lung diseases like bronchitis, emphysema, and pneumonia. However, it's not the nicotine itself that promotes long-term illness; it is the carcinogens, toxins, and particularly the tar that promote diseases.

Short-term effects:

PHYSICAL	PSYCHOLOGICAL
Increases heart rate	Over-release of neurotransmitters
Constricts blood vessels	(epinephrine, dopamine, norepinephrine)
Increases blood pressure	Changes in mood
Tachycardia (faster heart beat)	Euphoria

Arrhythmias (irregular heart beat)
Rise in body temperature
Restlessness
Anxiety, nervousness
Insomnia
Loss of appetite, weight loss
Rotted teeth
Gum disease
Tooth loss, broken teeth
Meth mouth
Nose bleeds
Gastrointestinal problems
Increases acne
Increases risk of heart attack and stroke

Mental confusion
Impaired judgment
Problems with decision-making
Loss of hand-eye coordination
Feelings of being indestructible
Irritability
Pressured speech, talkativeness
Paranoia
Psychosis (characterized by hallucinations and delusions)
Formication

Long-term effects:

PHYSICAL	PSYCHOLOGICAL
Weakened cardiovascular system	Brain damage
Complications from heart attack or stroke	Loss of neurons (nerve cells)
Heart disease	Loss of nerve pathways
Malnutrition	Memory loss
Cancers (of the mouth, lungs, throat, esophagus, larynx)	Cognitive deficits
Chronic lung disease, chronic bronchitis, pneumonia, emphysema (from smoking)	Depression
Premature aging	Possible dementia
	Paranoia
	Permanent psychosis

EXERCISE

Complete the chart and answer the questions that follow. Identify the stimulants you used, age of first use, number of times you experimented with drugs or frequency of use, and how you used the drugs.

IDENTIFY STIMULANTS YOU USED	AGE OF FIRST USE	NUMBER OF TIMES USED/ FREQUENCY: 1–5 Times Monthly, Weekly, Daily	ROUTE OF ADMINISTRATION: Snorting, Smoking, Oral, Injecting
Cocaine			
Crack Cocaine			
Amphetamines			
Meth/Crank			
Prescription Meds			
Nicotine			
Chewing Tobacco			
Ecstasy/MDMA			
Energy Drinks			
Other			

1. What short-term effects have you experienced?

   _____

   _____

2. What long-term effects, if any, have you experienced?

   _____

   _____

Group Exercises and Discussion Topics for Stimulants

GROUP EXERCISE AND DISCUSSION

If you choose, you can go online to download more information on specific stimulants, especially if there are certain drugs that the majority of group members have used. Print out copies of the information and have group members take turns reading it out loud. (If they don't want to read, you may choose to give readers an incentive—gum or candy, for example—which can also be used as a relapse prevention tactic, thereby having two purposes). Read the information and discuss topics like the following:

- Coke vs. crack—similarities and differences in effects
- Coke vs. crack—the differences in how the legal system prosecutes and punishes drug-related crimes
- Cocaethylene—the dangers of mixing cocaine and alcohol
- Meth and tweaking
- Meth and meth mouth
- Meth and how it interferes with sleep and energy
- Dangers of meth labs on people and the environment
- Different types of prescription amphetamines (e.g., ADHD medications, diet pills, meds for narcolepsy)—their effects and their abuse
- Ecstasy and its short-term and long-term effects on the brain and body
- Nicotine addiction
- Cigarette ingredients—toxicity and the health effects
- Cigarettes—second-hand and third-hand smoke
- Stimulant abuse and the heart
- The brain's reward-pleasure center and stimulant abuse
- Dangers of energy drinks
- How stimulants affect the teenage brain

GROUP DISCUSSION

Discuss as a group what stimulants individuals have used and the short- and long-term effects they have experienced.

GROUP EXERCISE AND DISCUSSION: MOVIE

Watch the movie *Thank You for Smoking* (2006), a satire with an anti-smoking message that is informative and educational. (Note: "R" rating.) After the movie, discuss the following:

- What were the advantages and disadvantages of smoking cigarettes depicted in the movie? Or put another way, what are the reasons to smoke and not to smoke cigarettes? What are the short-term and long-term effects of smoking on the brain and body?

- The cigarette industry targets youth. How was this depicted in the movie, and in what ways do they target youth? Why is it important to target teens as opposed to adults?

- What messages about addiction in general were communicated?

This exercise can be done individually or in groups or teams.

Directions:
Unscramble the letters to form words—types of stimulants or "uppers" (Hint: They are in alphabetical order.)

A R A D L D E L _____

B E L E T T U N S _____

E F A N C F I E _____

C H I N G E W   T A C C O O B _____

C A N O I C E _____

C C A R K _____

I D E T   I L L P S _____

S T E A C S Y _____

E R N Y G E   R D I K N S _____

I P H E R N D E E _____

M E P H E T A M M A T H E I N _____

C O N I T I N E _____

T A L I R I N _____

Answers:

ADDERALL

BETEL NUTS

CAFFEINE

CHEWING TOBACCO

COCAINE

CRACK

DIET PILLS

ECSTASY

ENERGY DRINKS

EPHEDRINE

METHAMPHETAMINE

NICOTINE

RITALIN

Depressants

What drugs are classified as depressants, and how do they affect the body and mind? Common depressants include:

- Alcohol
- Opium
- Morphine
- Codeine
- Heroin
- Prescription medications
- "Date-rape" drugs
- Methadone

Depressants generally depress and suppress body functions, but they also induce a high. Most depressants suppress pain, calm the body, reduce anxiety, and/or induce sleepiness. Depressants slow down body functions by reducing heart rate and blood pressure, slowing motor reflexes, relaxing the muscles, reducing respiration, and slowing cognitive functioning (thinking).

Some depressants are opiates, meaning they are derived from the opium poppy plant—like morphine and codeine—whereas others are more synthetic or man-made—like oxycontin. Opiates mimic the brain's own painkillers, endorphins and enkephalins, rendering the body's natural painkillers less efficient and effective after repeated use. Therefore, once users stop taking opiates and go into withdrawal, they often experience excessive pain and flu-like symptoms. Opiates also affect nerve cells in the limbic system, which controls emotion, as well as the brainstem and the spinal cord, both of which are involved in the pain response, body functions, and sensations (NIDA, 2011c).

Some prescription medications reduce anxiety and/or sedate the user. Two such medications may be referred to as "date-rape drugs" (rohypnol and gamma hydroxybutyrate (GHB)) as they have been used in the commission of sexual assaults and date rapes. They may be slipped into individuals' beverages without their knowledge, which causes sedation and incapacitation, making them more susceptible to sexual assault (NIDA, 2011d). Amnesia may result.

The most commonly used depressant is alcohol, which is covered in the next section.

Short-term effects:

PHYSICAL	PSYCHOLOGICAL
Reduced or suppressed pain	Reduced or suppressed emotional pain
Fatigue, sleepiness	Causes "high" or euphoria
Reduced anxiety/nervousness	Surge of pleasure

Stops diarrhea

Suppressed coughing

Slowed body functions and organs

Decreased heart rate

Decreased blood pressure

Lowered pulse

Slowed respiration

Initial sexual arousal

Loss of body heat

Slurred speech

Slowed cognitive functioning

Impaired decision-making

Impaired judgment

Loss of coordination

Memory loss

Long-term effects:

PHYSICAL	PSYCHOLOGICAL
Dependence	Reduction of natural dopamine
Decreased overall pain tolerance	Changes to limbic system, brain stem, and spinal cord
Inability for the body to fight its own pain	Mood disorders
Heart infections	
Heart-valve infections	
Chronic constipation	
Bacterial infections*	
Abscesses*	
Track marks*	
Collapsed veins*	
Contracting HIV, AIDS, Hepatitis*	

(*from IV drug use)

Complete the chart and answer the questions that follow. Identify the depressants you used, age of first use, number of times you experimented with drugs or frequency of use, and how you used the drugs.

IDENTIFY DEPRESSANTS YOU USED	AGE OF FIRST USE	NUMBER OF TIMES USED/ FREQUENCY: 1–5 Times Monthly, Weekly, Daily	ROUTE OF ADMINISTRATION: Snorting, Smoking, Oral, Injecting
Opium			
Morphine			
Codeine			
Heroin			
Prescription Meds			
"Date Rape" Drugs			
Methadone			
Other			

1. What short-term effects have you experienced?

    _____

    _____

2. Have you experienced withdrawal from depressants? If so, what symptoms did you experience (e.g., fever, pain, nausea)? Are they an incentive not to relapse?

_____

_____

3. What long-term effects, if any, have you experienced?

_____

_____

4. To your knowledge, have you ever been slipped a "date-rape drug" (e.g., GHB, "roofies") and then been taken advantage of in a sexual manner (e.g., raped, sexually assaulted, fondled)? What happened, and did you report it?

_____

_____

5. How did you cope with this? Did you see a therapist or contact a hotline?

_____

_____

Group Exercises and Discussion Topics for Depressants

GROUP EXERCISE AND DISCUSSION

You can go online to download more information on specific depressants, especially if there are certain drugs that the majority of group members have used. Print out copies of the information and have group members take turns reading it out loud. Again, you can offer candy or gum as an incentive. Read the information and discuss topics like the following:

- Prescription drug use and its effects in the short and long term
- Dangers of IV drug use
- Opium trade
- Importance of pain and the body's own system of painkillers (how endorphins and enkephalins work in pain suppression)

- Opiate withdrawal

- Heroin addiction

- Rising abuse of oxycontin

- Pros and cons of methadone maintenance

- Dangers of sleep medications (e.g., Ambien)

- Dangers of mixing depressants, and celebrities who have struggled with or died from this

GROUP DISCUSSION

Prescription drug use is on the rise. Have the group discuss their experiences using prescription drugs like painkillers, sedatives, anti-anxiety drugs, or even antidepressants. How did they acquire the drugs? Did they take pills from relatives who were prescribed the medications? Did they buy them online? Or were they prescribed the medications for a legitimate condition and then began to abuse them? What was their intent in using the drugs at first? How did prescription drug abuse affect their lives?

GROUP DISCUSSION

Rohypnol and GHB are widely considered "date-rape drugs" because they have been implicated in countless incidents of sexual assault. Have any in the group experienced this, and how has it changed their lives? Did they press charges or visit a doctor for a medical evaluation? How can they avoid this in the future, especially in college?

Alcohol

The most commonly used and socially acceptable depressant is alcohol. Alcohol derives from fermented grapes or grains, and may be consumed in beers (2–6 percent alcohol); wine, wine coolers, and champagne (8–20 percent); specific energy drinks (12 percent); and hard liquors (40–60 percent) (Foundation for a Drug Free World, 2009).

Alcohol affects males and females differently. The blood alcohol content (BAC) is the rate at which alcohol is eliminated from the body; .08 is the legal limit. Females tend to get drunk more quickly, in part because they have less water and more body fat, leading to the possibility of developing alcoholism more easily. Females are more likely to develop complications from alcohol use and are at higher risk for developing liver disease (e.g., cirrhosis), gastrointestinal problems, reproductive problems, hypertension and heart disease, and breast cancer (NIAAA, 2011a). Alcohol consumption during pregnancy can cause miscarriage, low birth weight, deformities, Fetal Alcohol Syndrome (FAS), FAS-related birth defects, and, later, learning disabilities (NIAAA, 2011b).

Alcohol initially creates a "buzz," but, as consumption increases and alcohol is absorbed into the blood stream, there are more depressant effects. Alcohol has numerous short-term and long-term effects on the body and brain in both sexes. Short-term effects include, but are not limited to, reduced heart rate, blood pressure, and pulse; muscle relaxation, slowed reflexes, and impaired motor coordination; slower organ functioning; impaired judgment; reduced alertness; depressed and/or negative mood; and, initially, reduced inhibitions (ADCAS, 2011a). Long-term effects include liver disease; heart disease; increased risk of heart attack, stroke, seizures, and coma; damage to the nervous system and brain; and cognitive impairments (ADCAS, 2011a; ADCAS, 2011b).

Short-term effects:

PHYSICAL	PSYCHOLOGICAL
Decreased heart rate	Lowered inhibitions and increased
Decreased blood pressure	sociability, initially
Lowered pulse	Over-release of serotonin and dopamine
Stimulates appetite	Increased aggressiveness
Induces sleep	Changes in mood
Muscle relaxation	Increased negative moods
Slowed motor reflexes	Exaggerated emotions
Slowed reaction time	Impaired judgment
Slowed overall organ functioning	Slurred speech
Loss of balance, clumsiness	Loss of hand-eye coordination
Impaired coordination	Slowed thinking overall
Flushing	Decreased concentration, focus, and attention
Blackouts	

Long-term effects:

PHYSICAL	PSYCHOLOGICAL
Liver disease (cirrhosis, hepatitis)	Atrophy (loss of brain tissue)
Gastrointestinal problems	Damage to nervous system
Heart disease	Aphasia (impairments in understanding or
High blood pressure	communicating language)
Heart attack	Dementia
Arrhythmia	Impaired memory
Stroke	Psychosis
Seizure	
Coma	
Malnutrition	
Vitamin deficiencies	
Anemia	
Reproductive problems	
Hormonal imbalance	
Osteoporosis	
Skin problems	
Breast cancer	
Fetal Alcohol Syndrome (increased risk if drinking while pregnant,)	

EXERCISE

Complete the chart and answer the questions that follow. Identify the alcoholic beverages you used, age of first use, number of times you experimented with alcohol or frequency of use, and how you obtained the alcohol (e.g., stole it from parents).

IDENTIFY ALCOHOLIC BEVERAGES YOU USED	AGE OF FIRST USE	NUMBER OF TIMES USED/ FREQUENCY: 1–5 Times Monthly, Weekly, Daily	HOW IT WAS OBTAINED
Beer			
Wine, Champagne			
Wine Coolers			
Alcoholic Energy Drinks			
Hard Liquor			
Other			

1. Have you experienced any short-term effects from drinking?

_____

_____

2. Have you experienced any long-term effects from drinking?

_____

_____

Group Exercises and Discussion Topics for Alcohol

GROUP EXERCISE AND DISCUSSION

You can go online to download more information on alcohol and its physical and psychological effects. Print out copies of the information and have group members take turns reading it out loud. Read the information and discuss topics like the following:

- Alcohol and its effects on the developing teenage brain

- Alcohol and liver disease

- Alcohol and the heart

- Alcohol and its effects on digestion, malnutrition, dehydration, and vitamin deficiency

- Fetal Alcohol Syndrome

- How alcohol affects females differently from males

- The dangers of mixing alcohol and medications

- Binge drinking in college

GROUP EXERCISE AND DISCUSSION

Identify and discuss the effects of drunk driving on individuals and communities as a whole. Explore physical/psychological, legal, and financial consequences. As group members identify the effects, write them on a board. If possible, invite a police officer to come to the group and discuss the legal effects of drunk driving. Many police departments have an officer who does presentations on drugs and the law.

GROUP DISCUSSION

Binge drinking is a type of substance abuse in which the drinker consumes a lot of alcohol in a relatively short period of time. Have members who have engaged in binge drinking describe their experiences. How often did this happen? In what kind of situations did they binge drink (e.g., parties, concerts, raves)? What preceded the decision to binge drink? What effects occurred as a result of binge drinking—for example, did they engage in behaviors (e.g., having sex, driving drunk, using drugs) in which they would not normally engage? What lessons can be learned about drinking?

GROUP EXERCISE: DEBATE

Should the legal age to drink be lowered to eighteen? Have everyone who answers yes to the question sit on one side of the room, and everyone who answers no on the other side facing the others, with a line down the middle of the room. Those who are undecided should sit on the end of the dividing line and may join either side at any time during the debate. Then debate the topic, making sure the adolescents raise their hands rather than blurting out their points. Only one speaker from each group should debate at a time, going back and forth. Some of the adolescents may change their minds and move their chairs to the other side. After a set period of time, stop the debate and see which side has the most adolescents. End by discussing how they felt debating the subject.

GROUP EXERCISE: ALCOHOL'S DOSAGE EFFECTS

This exercise can be done individually or in groups. You may turn it into a competitio
the person(s) who finish first, correctly.

Directions:

Here are seventeen physical, mental, and psychological effects of alcohol consumption. Five effects fall under each of the three categories. Two are not actual effects of alcohol on the body and brain. Place the effects (by letter) in the appropriate categories.

A. Mild sedation

B. Cirrhosis of the liver

C. Increased sociability

D. Blackouts and brownouts

E. Slurred speech

F. Hepatitis

G. Loss of balance and staggering

H. Anxiety

I. Heart disease and arrhythmias

J. Lowered inhibitions

K. Decreased alertness

L. Slowed digestion and absorption of nutrients

M. Malnutrition

N. Pain reduction

O. Mental clarity

P. Slowed reasoning and judgment

Q. Cancers of the esophagus, larynx, mouth, breast, and stomach

Low to moderate consumption:

1.

2.

3.

4

5.

High consumption, binge drinking, and overdose:

1.

2.

3.

4.

5.

Chronic high consumption/alcoholism:

1.

2.

3.

4.

5.

ANSWERS:

Low to moderate consumption:
1. A
2. C
3. J
4. N
5. P

High consumption, binge drinking, and overdose:
1. D
2. E
3. G
4. K
5. L

Chronic consumption/alcoholism:
1. B
2. F
3. I
4. M
5. Q

Hallucinogens/Psychedelics

What drugs are classified as hallucinogens/psychedelics, and how do they affect the body and mind? Common hallucinogens/psychedelics include:

- LSD (lysergic acid diethylamide)
- PCP (phencyclidine)
- DXM (dextromethorphan—found in cough syrups)
- Psilocybin, psilocin ("shrooms")
- Peyote (mescaline)
- Ibogaine
- Ketamine (may also be classified as a depressant)
- DMT (dimethyltryptamine)
- Salvia divinorum
- Nutmeg
- Mace
- Yage (ayahuasca)
- Morning glory seeds
- Inhalants, including nitrous oxide and whippets
- Marijuana, sinsemilla, hashish
- Spice

Hallucinogens (aka psychedelics) are a large class of drugs that primarily cause hallucinations and perceptual distortions (e.g., hearing or seeing things that are not real). They may also cause the following: synesthesia, the mixing of senses (e.g., seeing sounds, hearing colors); confusion; changes in emotion and mood; and dissociation or detachment (NIDA, 2010a; NIDA, 2001). Hallucinogens come in different forms.

- LSD, or lysergic acid diethylamide, comes from ergot, a fungus, and is typically taken orally via blotter paper.
- PCP, or phencyclidine, comes in powder, crystal, or liquid form.
- Psilocybin is the active ingredient in mushrooms (shrooms).
- Peyote, a cactus, has the active ingredient mescaline.

Other hallucinogens include:

- Ibogaine, an African shrub

- DMT (dimethyltryptamine), found in South American plants

- Salvia, a psychedelic plant grown in Mexico

- Yage, from vines in the Amazon jungle

- Morning glory seeds, found in ordinary gardens

Many have been used for centuries for religious and/or traditional purposes.

Another increasingly abused psychedelic is DXM, dextromethorphan, an active ingredient in many cough syrups and cough and cold medications (e.g., Coricidin), which are a quick and easy way to get high.

Short-term physical effects include increases in heart rate and blood pressure, rapid breathing, and elevated body temperature. It is the psychological effects, however, that are most striking. These include hallucinations, confusion, paranoia, dissociation/detachment, psychosis, coma, seizures, and Hallucinogen Persisting Perception Disorder (HPPD), in which the user has "trips" or flashbacks of use that occur spontaneously, and may occur long after use (NIDA, 2001).

Inhalants are another category of hallucinogens that include volatile solvents, or liquids that vaporize (e.g., paint thinners and removers, glues); aerosols or sprays (e.g., spray paints, hair sprays); gases (e.g., nitrous oxide); nitrates (e.g., amyl nitrate); and whippets (NIDA, 2010b). Inhalant use often precedes other substance abuse and peaks around age fourteen, but may produce life-threatening and lifelong effects, including severe brain damage, slower cognitive functioning, and problems with memory (NIDA 2010c).

Short-term effects:
(These are general short-term effects and may differ by substance.)

PHYSICAL	PSYCHOLOGICAL
Changes in heart rate and blood pressure	Hallucinations
Rapid breathing	Confusion
Increased temperature and sweating	Dizziness
Changes in appetite	Synesthesia
Dry mouth	Intensification of senses
Tremors	Detachment/dissociation
Agitation	Impaired thinking and judgment
Muscle contractions	Impaired coordination and movement
Nausea	Changes in mood and emotions
Vomiting	Paranoia
	Coma
	Psychosis

Long-term effects:

PHYSICAL	PSYCHOLOGICAL
Bone fractures (from severe muscle contractions)	Brain damage
Kidney damage	Permanent psychosis
	HPPD (with repeated flashbacks)
	Delirium
	Paranoia
	Depression

EXERCISE:

Complete the chart and answer the questions that follow. Identify the psychedelics you used, age of first use, number of times you used or frequency of use, and how you used the drugs.

IDENTIFY PSYCHEDELICS YOU USED	AGE OF FIRST USE	NUMBER OF TIMES USED/ FREQUENCY: 1–5 Times Monthly, Weekly, Daily	ROUTE OF ADMINISTRATION: Snorting, Smoking, Oral, Injecting
LSD			
PCP			
Shrooms (psilocybin)			
Peyote (mescaline)			
DMT			
Salvia			
DXM (cough syrups)			
Ketamine			
Ibogaine			
Inhalants, Whippets, Nitrous Oxide			
Marijuana, Sinsemilla, Hashish			
Spice			
Others: Yage, Morning Glory, Belladonna, Mace, Nutmeg			

1. What hallucinogens/psychedelics have you used? How often?

   _____

   _____

2. Have you experienced any short-term effects? If so, what?

   _____

   _____

3. Have you experienced any long-term effects? If so, what?

   _____

   _____

Group Exercises and Discussion Topics for Hallucinogens/Psychedelics

GROUP EXERCISE AND DISCUSSION

You can go online to download more information on specific hallucinogens, especially if there are certain drugs that the majority of group members have used. Print out copies of the information and have group members take turns reading it out loud. Read the information and discuss topics like the following:

- Psychological effects of LSD and/or PCP
- LSD and flashbacks, "bad trips"
- Abuse of cough syrups and cough and cold medications by teens
- Ketamine and veterinarians
- Use of ketamine as a date-rape drug
- DMT—what is it and why is it dangerous?
- Ibogaine—its use in the treatment of some addictions
- Inhalants as gateway drugs
- Dangers of inhalants
- Whippets and their effects (short-term and long-term) on the brain
- Spice—what it is and why teens are abusing it

GROUP EXERCISE: POLL

Take a poll in the group to see how their use of inhalants compares to the general school population. Ask the following:

- How many group members have used psychedelics?

- How many have used inhalants?

- At what age did group members begin huffing/using inhalants?

- How many of those who started huffing/using inhalants have gone on to use other drugs (including marijuana and alcohol)?

Discuss the findings. Ask for suggestions as to how to prevent inhalant use among teens.

GROUP DISCUSSION

Should psychedelics like peyote, yage, salvia, and psilocybin be legalized for religious/spiritual purposes? Discuss the pros and cons. Would legalizing these psychedelics increase their use and abuse?

GROUP DISCUSSION

Some professionals classify ecstasy as a psychedelic. What makes ecstasy a psychedelic (versus a stimulant), and should it be classified as such?

Marijuana

Marijuana is the most popular hallucinogen and is being used by more adolescents and p
cents at increasingly younger ages. Marijuana is typically smoked, although it can be taken orally, and comes from the cannabis plant. The active ingredient is delta-9-tetrahydrocannabinol (THC), which significantly effects several areas of the brain, including (but not limited to) the cerebral cortex (responsible for executive functioning, thinking, sensation, perception, and movement); the hippocampus (learning and memory); the cerebellum (coordination and movement); and the brain stem and spinal cord (sleep, arousal, sensation, reflexes) (NIDA, 2010c; Children's Hospital of Philadelphia, 2009). Research suggests that the earlier someone begins to smoke marijuana and the more someone uses, the greater the likelihood and extent of damage to the brain, particularly in speed of information processing, memory, executive functioning, and attention (Society for Neuroscience, 2010; Children's Hospital of Philadelphia, 2009). Marijuana use also reduces motivation, which can affect school and other activities.

Many adolescents believe that smoking marijuana isn't as dangerous or as harmful as smoking cigarettes, and that there are no long-term side-effects. This is false! Because the average marijuana smoker takes longer and deeper puffs than a cigarette smoker, the lungs, body, and blood are exposed to more carcinogens and toxins (e.g., ammonia, hydrogen cyanide, amines), and less oxygen is transported to the brain and heart (NIDA, 2010c; ACS, 2007). In turn, marijuana smokers are at greater risk for having a heart attack or stroke or developing cancer, respiratory problems, and lung infections (Molecular Psychiatry, 2008; Yale, 2007).

Short-term effects:

PHYSICAL	PSYCHOLOGICAL
Increased heart rate	Hallucinations
Increased blood pressure	Impaired judgment
Increased pulse	Impaired short-term memory
Cotton mouth	Impaired verbal memory
Increased appetite	Impaired cognitive functioning
Coughing	Impaired coordination and movement
Increased phlegm	Imbalance
Pain control	Slowed reaction time
	Altered sensory perception
	Psychosis
	Delusions

Long-term effects:

PHYSICAL	PSYCHOLOGICAL
Increased risk of lung infections	Impaired memory
Increased risk of chronic respiratory problems (e.g., bronchitis)	Increased risk of depression
	Increased risk of schizophrenia
Increased risk of cancers of the head, neck, lungs, mouth, throat	Psychosis
	Amotivational syndrome (reduced motivation)

EXERCISE:

Answer the following questions:

1. At what age did you first try marijuana? What about other psychedelics? What were the circumstances, and do you think trying marijuana opened the door for other substance use?

   _____

   _____

2. What short-term effects have you experienced from marijuana or other psychedelics?

   _____

   _____

3. What long-term effects, if any, have you experienced from psychedelics?

   _____

   _____

4. Marijuana can have dramatic or subtle effects on motivation. How has your motivation to do things (i.e., go to school, play sports, etc.) changed? Has your motivation decreased since you began using marijuana?

   _____

   _____

Group Exercises and Discussion Topics for Marijuana

GROUP EXERCISE: DOCUMENTARY

Have the group watch the documentary *The Truth About Drugs: Real People Real Stories* (Foundation for a Drug-Free World, 2009), which discusses the effects of different drugs, beginning with marijuana. The documentary contains facts on substances and individuals discuss their negative experiences, including how drugs affected their lives physically, emotionally, socially, educationally, and financially. This documentary is a good way to end the drug education portion. Discuss in depth afterward, as individuals in the group may be affected by the contents. Discuss the following:

- What were the themes or messages of the documentary? What were the messages around addiction, recovery, and prevention?

- To what or to whom can group members relate? Why, or in what way(s)?

- Was their drug(s) of choice discussed? If so, could they relate to what the individuals in the movie said about the drug(s)?

- Was there anything they learned about drugs? If so, what?

- Did this video trigger the urge to use through its discussion of drugs, or was it more of a motivator to live clean and sober? For those who feel triggered to use, this opens up the topic of self-care and how to care for themselves when triggered. What can group members do to manage the triggers and cravings?

GROUP DISCUSSION

One side-effect of marijuana use is reduced motivation. This often shows up in school or outside activities—feeling unmotivated to attend classes or complete schoolwork, or to participate in sports and other after-school activities. Have individual group members experienced a loss in motivation since they began using marijuana? How has this affected their lives and their overall drug use? Discuss.

GROUP DISCUSSION

One controversial topic is the addictive potential of marijuana. Some researchers argue that marijuana is not addictive and that users do not go through withdrawal when they cease using. Other researchers argue that there is an addictive potential and that chronic users can, in fact, experience tolerance and withdrawal symptoms. What do group members think? Have them consider this from both an individual perspective and in terms of substance abusers as a whole. Discuss.

GROUP EXERCISE: DEBATE

Should marijuana be legalized? Have everyone who answers yes to the question sit on one side of the room, and everyone who answers no on the other side facing the others, with a line down the middle of the room. Those who are undecided should sit on the end of the dividing line and may join either side at any time during the debate. Then debate the topic, making sure the adolescents raise their hands rather than blurting out their points. Only one speaker from each group should debate at a time, going back and forth. Some of the adolescents may change their minds and move their chairs to the other side. After a set period of time, stop the debate and see which side has the most adolescents. End by discussing how they felt debating the subject.

3

Identifying Patterns of Use

Setting and Achieving Goals in Recovery

Treatment and recovery from substance abuse/addiction may be one of the most difficult experiences in your life. Setting (and achieving) goals makes treatment and recovery a bit easier, more manageable, and less overwhelming. Setting and working toward achieving your goals keeps you on track, tells you where you are in the recovery process, and gives you purpose. When you achieve your goals—small and big—it boosts your self-esteem and self-confidence. Recovery is a slow process that requires taking little baby steps on a daily basis with short-term and long-term goals.

Short-term goals should be:

- Positive and healthy

- Simple and uncomplicated

- Specific

- Do-able (achievable)

- Realistic

Short-term goals should be made on a daily basis and evaluated either at the end of the day or the following morning. Short-term goals should also be made weekly and evaluated once a week. Short-term goals may work up to meeting a long-term goal; hence, short-term goals are the baby steps.

Long-term goals should be:

- Do-able

- Realistic

- Beneficial in the long run

- Enhance recovery

This exercise is to be completed over the course of one week. At the beginning of each day (or the night before), set a daily goal, keeping in mind the short-term guidelines. At the end of each day, evaluate your goal and whether or not you achieved it. Note the obstacles you struggled with to achieve the goals, which may be external (e.g., transportation issues, logistics, lack of money) or internal (e.g., laziness, procrastination).

DAY 1:

Goal: _____

_____

Did I achieve my goal?_____

Obstacles: _____

_____

How I Managed the Obstacles: _____

_____

DAY 2:

Goal: _____

_____

Did I achieve my goal?_____

Obstacles: _____

_____

How I Managed the Obstacles: _____

_____

DAY 3:

Goal: _____

_____

Did I achieve my goal? _____

Obstacles: _____

_____

How I Managed the Obstacles: _____

_____

DAY 4:

Goal: _____

_____

Did I achieve my goal? _____

Obstacles: _____

_____

How I Managed the Obstacles: _____

_____

DAY 5:

Goal: _____

_____

Did I achieve my goal? _____

Obstacles: _____

_____

How I Managed the Obstacles: _____

_____

DAY 6:

Goal: _____
_____

Did I achieve my goal?_____

Obstacles: _____
_____

How I Managed the Obstacles: _____
_____

DAY 7:

Goal: _____
_____

Did I achieve my goal?_____

Obstacles: _____
_____

How I Managed the Obstacles: _____
_____

This is to be completed once a week for four weeks. At the start of the week, write down a goal you will be working on achieving throughout the week, keeping in mind the guidelines. After one week, evaluate your goal, noting whether or not you achieved it. Rate how effective you were in achieving this goal on a scale of 1 to 10 (1 = not effective at all; 10 = maximum effectiveness). Note the steps you took to achieve the goal. Then note the obstacles and how you managed them.

WEEK 1:	STEPS I TOOK:
GOAL:	OBSTACLES:
DID I ACHIEVE MY GOAL? EFFECTIVENESS RATING:	HOW I MANAGED THE OBSTACLES:

WEEK 2:	STEPS I TOOK:
GOAL:	OBSTACLES:
DID I ACHIEVE MY GOAL? EFFECTIVENESS RATING:	HOW I MANAGED THE OBSTACLES:

WEEK 3:	STEPS I TOOK:
GOAL:	OBSTACLES:
DID I ACHIEVE MY GOAL? EFFECTIVENESS RATING:	HOW I MANAGED THE OBSTACLES:

WEEK 4:	STEPS I TOOK:
GOAL:	OBSTACLES:
DID I ACHIEVE MY GOAL? EFFECTIVENESS RATING:	HOW I MANAGED THE OBSTACLES:

Group Discussion Topics for Setting and Achieving Goals in Recovery

GROUP DISCUSSION

Have group members share some of their daily goals and whether or not they achieved them. How did this feel? Were they motivated to achieve their goals, and what motivated them? Did achieving goals motivate them, or were they motivated more by their "failure" to achieve goals? How does this relate to their substance abuse, and to life in general?

GROUP DISCUSSION

Have group members share their weekly goals, and whether or not they achieved their goals from the last week. Were their goals positive, simple, specific, do-able, and realistic? Have those who achieved their goals explain how they accomplished this. What strategies did they use? For those who did not meet their goals, have them focus on what they did to work toward achieving their goals—the positives—as opposed to what they didn't do. How does this feel?

GROUP DISCUSSION

Have group members think back to a time before they began using drugs. What were their goals, aspirations, or dreams, and how different are they from now? How have these changed, and what part did drugs play in this change? Are they more or less motivated now?

Gateway Drugs and Stages of Use

Substance use occurs in stages—beginning with experimentation, followed by recreational (or social) use, habituation, substance abuse, and addiction. It may progress rapidly or slowly, depending on different variables. The first stage is *experimentation,* in which an individual tries one or more drugs for various reasons, including curiosity and peer pressure. This may begin with "gateway drugs" that open doors to the use of other drugs. Common gateway drugs are alcohol, marijuana, and nicotine.

Sometimes experimentation can lead to *recreational (or social) use*—drinking with friends at a dinner party, for example. For many individuals, substance use never goes beyond recreational use, but for some who have a genetic predisposition to addiction, family problems, personal problems, or poor coping skills, it may progress further.

Habituation occurs when substance use becomes a pattern and can escalate to *substance abuse,* or misuse. An individual may continue to use substances in dangerous or risky situations—for example, drinking and driving or injecting with needles—engaging in behaviors in which they may not otherwise have engaged.

When substance abuse continues to escalate and becomes a pattern of continued use despite the negative consequences, it can lead to *addiction.* Two characteristics of addiction are tolerance, needing increased amounts of a given substance to get the same effect, and the presence of withdrawal symptoms when the drugs begin to wear off. At this point, detoxification and treatment may be necessary.

EXERCISE

Answer the following questions to trace your use. Identify the substances with which you have experimented.

1._____   6._____
2._____   7._____
3._____   8._____
4._____   9._____
5._____   10._____

Circle the substance(s) that you believe was your gateway drug(s).

Identify the drug(s) you used recreationally/socially:

1._____   6._____
2._____   7._____
3._____   8._____
4._____   9._____
5._____   10._____

Identify risky or potentially harmful situations in which you used substances, and dangerous behaviors in which you have engaged while using. Examples include drinking and driving or sharing needles while shooting up.

1._____
2._____
3._____
4._____
5._____
6._____

What were the drugs you abused/misused in these risky situations?

1._____   6._____
2._____   7._____
3._____   8._____
4._____   9._____
5._____   10._____

Looking back at the situations you identified as risky or potentially risky, are you surprised at your responses? Did you use in more risky situations than you previously thought? Are you surprised at the situations you put yourself in while using?

_____
_____

What was the most risky situation in which you used, and what were the consequences?

_____
_____

As a clean and sober person, would you engage in this behavior? Why or why not?

_____
_____

Given your answers and what you know about addiction, would you say you have substance addiction? To what drug(s)? Did all of this begin with a gateway drug?

_____

_____

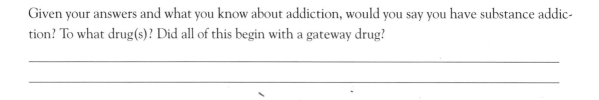

Group Discussion Topics for Gateway Drugs and Stages of Use

GROUP DISCUSSION

What is a gateway drug, and what qualifies a drug to be labeled a gateway drug? Some group members may disagree with the entire concept of gateway drugs and argue that there is no such thing because it's all about willpower and choice. Others may argue that gateway drugs open the door to other drug use, and that's their only quality. Still others may believe that there are other qualities that make a drug a gateway drug. Discuss how group members define gateway drugs, and whether or not they believe the following drugs are gateway drugs:

- Nicotine (cigarettes)
- Alcohol
- Marijuana

GROUP DISCUSSION

Have each group member go through their stages of use and identify the following:

- The drugs with which they experimented
- The drugs they used recreationally/socially
- The drugs they abused and any patterns of drug use
- The drugs to which they are addicted, if any

Have each individual share how his or her drug use progressed from experimentation to substance abuse or addiction. What was common among group members? Discuss.

GROUP DISCUSSION

There is an argument that taxing gateway drugs like nicotine reduces the number of people who smoke cigarettes—that people are more likely to quit smoking due to the high prices. Taxes on nicotine, for example, are then used to cover the medical costs of smokers as they age and develop smoking-related diseases (e.g., emphysema, lung cancer). Given this argument, should alcohol be taxed highly? Some cities are playing with this idea.

Cycle of Substance Addiction

For many substance abusers, the cycle of use develops into a cycle of addiction. While it is important to note that not everyone in formal treatment or recovery is an addict, everyone who abuses drugs has the potential to become addicted. Substance addiction is a cyclical process that takes time to develop into a pattern that can spiral downward, much like a tornado, if the addict does not try to stop it or prevent it.

The cycle of substance addiction begins with a trigger (person, place, object, feeling, thought, or behavior) that provokes the urge or craving to use. We will be looking more closely at triggers in the next section and identifying personal triggers. Triggers lead to a period of building tension in which thoughts, feelings, attitudes, and behaviors may grow increasingly negative or problematic. Warning signs—changes in behaviors, thoughts, and feelings—of a possible relapse may appear, coupled with an internal struggle between giving in to those desires to use and fighting off the tension. Additionally, there may be an increase in high-risk behaviors.

Eventually, addicts will relapse if they don't take steps to counteract the triggers and warning signs with more positive coping skills. A relapse is different for everyone, but is generally considered to be a return to substance use and old behaviors—drinking alcohol, snorting coke, huffing paint thinner, or using painkillers to get high, for example.

The relapse may induce feelings of regret, remorse, embarrassment, and/or shame. Addicts may make (false) promises to themselves and to others to change and get back on track by attending 12-Step meetings, seeing a counselor, and practicing coping skills to stay clean and sober. They may make promises of abstinence, saying "I'll never use again." They may subsequently feel better and stronger.

However, if the addict does not continue to practice these coping skills, this phase may be short-lived, and will eventually begin another cycle of use with the introduction of a new trigger. Thus, the cycle repeats itself.

CYCLE OF ADDICTION

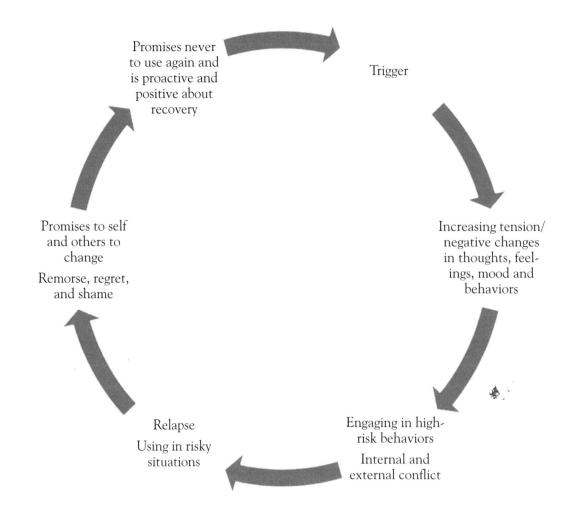

Promises never to use again and is proactive and positive about recovery

Trigger

Increasing tension/ negative changes in thoughts, feelings, mood and behaviors

Promises to self and others to change

Remorse, regret, and shame

Relapse

Using in risky situations

Engaging in high-risk behaviors

Internal and external conflict

Evaluate yourself and your pattern of substance use by answering the following questions:

1. How do you know you've been triggered? How do cravings and urges to use feel in your body? For example, do you grow anxious or do your hands get clammy?

    _____

    _____

    _____

2. Following exposure to a trigger, tension builds and warning signs begin to emerge. Warning signs are changes in feelings, thoughts, behaviors, attitudes, and moods that indicate someone is in relapse mode. What are your warning signs?

    _____

    _____

    _____

3. With increasing tension, the addict experiences internal and external conflict. Internal conflict may take the form of dialogue in the head: "use," "don't use," "use," "don't use . . ." Or "using feels good," vs. "using is bad for me." What internal conflict do you experience?

    _____

    _____

    _____

4. External conflict may take the form of increased arguing, for example. What external conflict do you experience before relapsing?

    _____

    _____

    _____

5. What does a relapse look like for you? Is it drinking one sip of alcohol, smoking a cigarette, smoking a blunt, or shooting heroin? To what extent do you consider a relapse a relapse?

    _____

    _____

    _____

6. What do you feel or would you expect to feel after a relapse? Shame? Regret? Guilt? Embarrassment?

_____

_____

_____

7. If you relapsed, what would you do to get back on track?

_____

_____

_____

8. To whom could you be accountable, or on whom could you rely for help in getting clean and sober again?

_____

_____

_____

_____

Group Exercises and Discussion Topics for the Cycle of Substance Addiction

GROUP DISCUSSION

Study the cycle of substance abuse/addiction. Discuss the following aspects of the cycle:

- *Triggers.* What are triggers? How do they provoke the urge to use? What are some triggers common among members of the group?

- *Warning signs.* What are the warning signs people identified, and will the introduction of coping skills stop the cycle or prevent the relapse?

- *Internal and external conflict.* What is the internal conflict going on in the addict's head, and how is this acted out externally? What are the conflicting messages that addicts struggle with internally?

- *Relapse.* What is the difference between a "lapse" and a relapse? Is there a difference, and is one worse than the other?

- *Where can you stop the cycle, and how?* What are the clean-and-sober coping skills people in the group are learning and practicing? Explore coping skills to break the cycle.

GROUP DISCUSSION

Addiction can be physiological or psychological. Have the group explore the similarities and differences between physiological and psychological dependence (addiction).

GROUP EXERCISE AND DISCUSSION

On a board or sheet of butcher paper, write "Relapse Prevention." Ask the group what relapse means and what it looks like. Some individuals may say it's merely using a drug, but that is only one aspect of relapse. Relapse is a pattern of thoughts, behaviors, attitudes, and feelings. Have group members come up to the board and write words and phrases describing what they consider to be relapse. They should conclude from this part of the exercise that relapse is a process. Then, ask them to list what prevention includes (also a process). They can list anything from building coping skills, to anger management, to support groups or meetings or groups, etc. Combine both. Hence the term "Relapse Prevention." This puts together all the exercises, groups, and therapeutic processes involved in treatment.

Challenge the group to identify and list thirty coping skills they can use to get back on track after a relapse. Coping skills are proactive behaviors that enable the substance abuser or addict to stay clean and sober. (*Examples:* Journaling, talking to a friend, playing football.)

NA/AA meeting. _____ _____ _____

_____ _____ _____

_____ _____ _____

_____ _____ _____

_____ _____ _____

_____ _____ _____

_____ _____ _____

_____ _____ _____

_____ _____ _____

_____ _____ _____

_____ _____ _____

_____ _____ _____

_____ _____ _____

_____ _____ _____

_____ _____ _____

Triggers

Identify all the people, places, objects, feelings/emotions, thoughts, and behaviors that trigger your desire or craving to use substances. Be as specific as possible. The goal is to identify as many triggers as possible and to develop coping skills to manage these triggers, thereby preventing relapse. Examples are given.

PEOPLE	PLACES	OBJECTS/THINGS
Examples:	*Examples:*	*Examples:*
Friends who use	Liquor stores	Bongs
Drug dealers	Parks	Bottles
Celebrities	Parties	Pipes

FEELINGS/ EMOTIONS	THOUGHTS	BEHAVIORS
Examples: Anger Boredom Sadness	*Examples:* Negative Thoughts ("I am stupid.") Pessimistic Thoughts ("Everything's Bad.") Suicidal Thoughts ("I want to die.")	*Examples:* Fighting Partying Smoking

Group Exercises and Discussion Topics for Triggers

GROUP EXERCISE

In small groups or teams of two, role play situations in which triggers may create the urge to use; then model ineffective versus effective ways of coping with the triggers. Discuss these differences in coping responses.

GROUP EXERCISE AND DISCUSSION

Divide the group into teams and have the teams compete to identify the most triggers. Go through and discuss each category of triggers.

GROUP DISCUSSION

Discuss how triggers trigger cravings, and how individuals experience cravings. Are the cravings experienced on a physical level—for example, does your mouth water? Do your hands shake? Does your body temperature change? Or are the cravings psychological—for example, do you keep telling yourself you need the substance, can't function normally without it, or can't have fun without it? Are the cravings experienced emotionally—for example, do your moods change suddenly or dramatically?

GROUP DISCUSSION

Substances can be replaced with negative behaviors, leading to the possible development of process addictions. These behaviors may occur in conjunction with drug abuse, or in place of drug abuse. Process addictions include:

- Gambling addiction/problem gambling
- Eating disorders (e.g., compulsive binge eating, binge-and-purge eating, starving)
- Sex addiction
- Addiction to pornography or Internet porn
- Self-harming (e.g., cutting or burning yourself)
- Shopping addiction
- Hoarding

Some may associate these behaviors with feelings of relief or release, and, like substance use, these can be learned and un-learned. Have group members discuss their own problem behaviors/ process addictions. Explore triggers to these behaviors and why they use these behaviors. Identify alternative responses. If group members do not display compulsive behaviors, consider family members (e.g., parents), whose behaviors can open the doorway to these problem behaviors.

Triggers and Coping Responses

Now that you have identified triggers—people, places, objects/things, feelings/emotions, thoughts, behaviors—that may trigger the urge or cravings to use, it is important to identify ways of coping with these triggers as well. Coping strategies are diverse, but should generally be positive, healthy, and, depending on the needs of the individual, relaxing and/or energizing. Exercise, sports, and physical activity may help ward off anxiety, for example, and may create an adrenaline rush—a "natural high" to take the place of getting high on a drug. On the other hand, meditating, journaling, or reading may prove more relaxing to others. Distraction is one type of coping strategy, as hobbies, activities, and interests can help refocus attention on positive pursuits, reducing compulsive thoughts of using.

It is important to identify, acknowledge, and experience these feelings. Often, if you let yourself feel the anger or sadness underneath the urge, it reduces the desire to use. Socializing or "hanging out" with people who understand what it is like to have cravings and urges to use at meetings or social gatherings may be most helpful to some individuals. "Getting back" to peers through talking, texting, calling, or even singing can be therapeutic. Remember: The goal of coping strategies is to prevent relapse. Or, if you have already relapsed, they can help you regain a clean and sober lifestyle.

EXERCISE

List as many interests (e.g., skateboarding, video games), hobbies (e.g., painting, cooking), or strengths/abilities (e.g., making friends, drawing, playing basketball) as possible. All are sources of coping.

_____ _____

_____ _____

_____ _____

_____ _____

_____ _____

_____ _____

_____ _____

Identify triggers in each of the categories—people, places, objects/things, feelings/emotions, thoughts, behaviors—and two ways of coping with each trigger. You may want to refer back to the charts in the Triggers section.

Example: Parties—(A) leave the situation; (B) go to a NA/AA meeting
Example: Sadness—(A) talk to a friend or supportive person; (B) journal

People:

_____ (A)_____ (B)_____
_____ (A)_____ (B)_____
_____ (A)_____ (B)_____
_____ (A)_____ (B)_____
_____ (A)_____ (B)_____

Places:

_____ (A)_____ (B)_____
_____ (A)_____ (B)_____
_____ (A)_____ (B)_____
_____ (A)_____ (B)_____
_____ (A)_____ (B)_____

Objects:

_____ (A)_____ (B)_____
_____ (A)_____ (B)_____
_____ (A)_____ (B)_____
_____ (A)_____ (B)_____
_____ (A)_____ (B)_____

Feelings/Emotions:

_____ (A)_____ (B)_____
_____ (A)_____ (B)_____
_____ (A)_____ (B)_____
_____ (A)_____ (B)_____
_____ (A)_____ (B)_____

Thoughts:

_____ (A)_____ (B)_____
_____ (A)_____ (B)_____
_____ (A)_____ (B)_____
_____ (A)_____ (B)_____
_____ (A)_____ (B)_____

Behaviors:

_____ (A)_____ (B)_____
_____ (A)_____ (B)_____
_____ (A)_____ (B)_____
_____ (A)_____ (B)_____
_____ (A)_____ (B)_____

Group Exercise and Discussion Topics for Triggers and Coping Responses

GROUP DISCUSSION

Why is it important to identify and participate in positive interests? How does this affect overall motivation? What are some examples of positive interests individuals in the group identified? What about identifying strengths and abilities? How do these affect overall recovery?

GROUP DISCUSSION

Many triggers are situational, like parties, raves, or clubs. One strategy may be to avoid or leave the situation, which in most cases is probably the "safer" response. However, some may argue that we need to challenge ourselves in these situations by developing skills and alternatives to cope with them rather than "running away" from them. For example, should alcoholics avoid bars or liquor stores altogether, or purposely challenge their strength and resolve by going into bars and liquor stores? Discuss the pros and cons of avoiding such situational triggers versus testing yourself. Which seems to be the "safer" alternative and why?

GROUP DISCUSSION

Some people may argue that coping is different from healing and that coping skills don't go far enough. Coping may be defined as using strategies to solve or manage a problem, whereas healing involves processing or working through the underlying emotions at a deeper level. Have the group discuss the difference, if any, between coping and healing in the recovery process.

Have each member of the group practice coping with triggers they have identified in the period of time between groups. For example, seeing someone smoke a cigarette may be an identified trigger—one they may not be able to plan for. Let's say an individual is walking down the street and sees someone smoking, which triggers the urge to smoke (or use). This is an opportunity to practice the coping skills he or she may have identified. After doing so in the next group, evaluate whether the coping skills the person used worked to reduce the urge to use or prevent relapse. Group members need to be aware of all the triggers and coping skills they have used in the period of time between groups. They may want to write them down so that they can discuss them in the next group.

12-Step Work

One major coping skill is grounded in the 12 Steps. Many individuals and treatment programs utilize the 12 Steps in the recovery process, and no relapse prevention plan would be complete without them. The 12 Steps are the foundation of support networks like Alcoholics Anonymous (AA) and Narcotics Anonymous (NA). There are many advantages to attending AA or NA meetings and/or working the 12 Steps. Meetings are generally available any time of the day or night, 365 days a year. Individuals can build a support network of fellow substance abusers/addicts who can relate to what they are going through and support them in the recovery process. There is a vast array of literature on the 12 Steps, including the "Big Book." You can choose to work through the 12 Steps with the help of a sponsor, which may be a very rewarding and life-altering process. The 12 Steps can be summarized as follows (Alcoholics Anonymous, 2001):

Steps 1–3 generally focus on admitting that you have a problem with substances, admitting powerlessness over drugs and alcohol, pledging to be honest with yourself in this process, developing a readiness to change, and putting your faith in a Higher Power because life has become "unmanageable."

Steps 4–9 focus on identifying, acknowledging, and compensating for the ways in which you have hurt others and yourself.

Steps 10–12 focus on the idea of giving back—practicing what you have learned and offering to help others through their struggle.

It's important to understand that the 12 Steps and 12-Step groups are not affiliated with any religious organizations or religions. Moreover, the Higher Power that individuals acknowledge may be anything of their choosing, as long as it is something greater than them in which they have faith—for example, God, Allah, the Buddha, angels, Mother Nature, the universe, or even AA.

EXERCISE
Answer the following questions based on Steps 1, 2, and 3, which are the foundation of the 12 Steps.

1. According to Alcoholics Anonymous (2001, p.59), Step 1 states: "We admitted we were powerless over alcohol [and/or drugs]—that our lives had become unmanageable." The key word is powerless. What does this first step mean to you?

   _____

   _____

   _____

   _____

What does it mean to you to be powerless over alcohol or drugs? Do you think you are powerless over alcohol and/or drugs? Why or why not?

_____

_____

_____

What does it mean to you to admit that your life is unmanageable? Think of all the ways in which your life has become unmanageable due to drugs and/or alcohol and list them.

_____

_____

_____

2. Step 2 states: "[We] came to believe that a Power greater than ourselves could restore us to sanity" (AA, 2001, p. 59). This step introduces us to the idea of a Higher Power, which can take many forms. The Higher Power is just something bigger than you that may take any form like God, Yahweh, the universe, or AA. What do you consider to be your Higher Power, and why?

_____

_____

_____

Putting their faith in a Higher Power may be intimidating or scary for some people. Others may be turned off by the whole idea of spirituality in recovery. It is important to note that a Higher Power is a spiritual concept, not a religious one. How do you define spirituality, and what role do you want spirituality to take in your recovery?

_____

_____

_____

3. Step 3 states: "[We] made a decision to turn our will and our lives over to the care of God _as we understood Him_" (AA, 2001, p.59). Step 3 is about commitment and a decision to put control in the hands of our Higher Power. Step 1 involves admitting we have a problem, while Step 3 calls us to make a commitment to take action. Do you feel you are committed to the recovery process? Why or why not?

_____

_____

_____

What does commitment look like to you? How does this relate to understanding your Higher Power?

_____

_____

EXERCISE

Go online and find a list of AA or NA meetings in your area, and attend a meeting. Then evaluate your experience.

Meeting Date & Time:_____

Location:_____

Answer the following questions based on your attendance at an AA or NA meeting:

1. Describe the group. Was it an AA or NA meeting? Was it a topical, 12-Step, or storytelling group? Was it for adolescents or open to addicts of any age? How many people attended the group? (Do not report what was discussed, as that is confidential.)

_____

_____

_____

2. Did attendees share their stories of addiction? Were there parts of their stories to which you could relate? How did it make you feel hearing their stories and/or relating to them? (Do not report the stories, as that is confidential.)

_____

_____

_____

3. Before or after the group, did people come up to you and introduce themselves? (Do not give names, as that is confidential.) Did you feel the atmosphere was friendly, as if people were really trying to help each other? Did anyone talk about sponsorship?

_____

_____

4. What was your overall impression of the group? Is this a group you would be willing to attend again? Why or why not?

_____

_____

_____

Group Exercise and Discussion Topics for 12-Step Work

GROUP DISCUSSION

Discuss each of the 12 Steps in detail to better understand them and what they mean. How might someone begin to work the 12 Steps?

GROUP DISCUSSION

Admitting and accepting powerlessness over alcohol and/or drugs is fundamental to the 12 Steps and recovery. Have the group explore how they define powerlessness and what it means to be powerless over substances. Who in the group has admitted to and accepted their powerlessness over substances, and what did it take to get to that place? Are some group members still be in denial or unwilling to accept they have a problem? Discuss how someone can move to a place of accepting of his or her powerlessness.

GROUP DISCUSSION

Steps 4–9 focus on acknowledging how we have affected others by our addictive behaviors, accounting for the ways in which we have hurt others, and compensating, or "righting those wrongs." Compensation takes many forms. We may apologize for our behaviors, pay restitutions or fines, and fix or replace what is broken, physically and emotionally. What do group members think about this? Give individuals a chance to acknowledge and take responsibility for their behaviors, and have the group strategize how they can compensate. Allow for feedback and processing of emotions, as this may be difficult for some.

GROUP DISCUSSION

The idea of a Higher Power can be controversial. What do group members think about the concept of the Higher Power as discussed in the 12 Steps? How do they define a Higher Power? What are the possibilities? Do individuals believe in a Higher Power and, if so, what do they identify as such? Who doesn't believe in a Higher Power, and why?

GROUP DISCUSSION

Explore the differences between religion and spirituality. Some people may be uncomfortable with the whole Higher Power concept, which is more spiritual and actually has little if anything to do with religion. Discuss the difference between religion and spirituality, and the role of spirituality in the recovery process in general.

GROUP EXERCISE: HOMEWORK ASSIGNMENT

Have the group members read the first four chapters of the *Big Book,* which discusses Bill's Story and the founding ideas behind Alcoholics Anonymous and alcoholism. Then discuss each of the chapters.

4

Preventing Relapse

Warning Signs

Feelings, thoughts, and behaviors can be further impacted by attitudes, which often become more negative and pessimistic before a relapse, and more optimistic and positive when you are clean and sober. This brings us to the topic of warning signs—changes in attitudes, feelings, thoughts, and behaviors that may alert substance abusers/addicts to an impending relapse. Changes commonly include an increase in impulsive or negative behaviors and the growing use of excuses or justifications for these changes in behaviors.

EXERCISE
Complete the following exercises to identify your warning signs.

1. Changes in feelings that may be warning signs include:

    Examples:
    Feeling sad more often
    Feeling hopeless
    Inability to feel feelings

    _____   _____
    _____   _____
    _____   _____
    _____   _____
    _____   _____
    _____   _____

2. Changes in thoughts—actual statements or beliefs we tell ourselves or thought patterns we repeat—that may be warning signs include:

   Examples:
   Thinking "I have to have drugs to have fun"
   Thinking "I have to have drugs to feel normal"
   Pessimistic thinking
   Suicidal thoughts

   _____   _____
   _____   _____
   _____   _____
   _____   _____
   _____   _____

3. Changes in behaviors that may be warning signs include:

   Examples:
   Skipping school
   Hanging out with friends who use
   Lying to parents

   _____   _____
   _____   _____
   _____   _____
   _____   _____
   _____   _____

4. Changes in attitudes, demeanor, and moods that may be warning signs include:

   Examples:
   Negative attitude
   Depressed mood

   _____   _____
   _____   _____
   _____   _____
   _____   _____
   _____   _____

Group Exercises and Discussion Topics for Warning Signs

GROUP DISCUSSION

What are some of the changes in feelings, thoughts, attitudes, and behaviors that may signal impending relapse? Write these warning signs on a board and see how many individuals in the group relate to them. Are these warning signs under our locus of control? Are they under the control of individual group members? Or are they outside our locus of control? Are they due to someone else? Discuss.

GROUP DISCUSSION

Some warning signs of relapse may be very subtle and simple, like not making your bed in the morning, not cleaning up after yourself, or avoiding supportive people (like a therapist or sponsor). What are some of these subtle warning signs that group members identify? Why could these warning signs progress to relapse? Are these signs due to a lack of awareness, or laziness, or some other factor? Why is awareness important in recovery?

GROUP EXERCISE

Identify the ten most popular warning signs group members listed. Have the group make a poster of the top ten warning signs and how to counteract them. Discuss. Has anyone in the group experienced these changes recently, and how did they deal with them? Leave the poster up for each group as a topic of discussion and reminder of what to look for.

GROUP EXERCISE: HOMEWORK ASSIGNMENT

Have group members share their warning signs with family members and friends to whom they can be accountable in recovery. They may choose to share their warning signs in a family therapy session where the discussion can be moderated by a counselor. Then, at the next group session, the group members can share what this was like and discuss their experiences or process any feelings that came up.

Defense Mechanisms

All human beings use defense mechanisms—psychological strategies we use for self-preservation. When our self-esteem, self-concept, or self-identity seem threatened, we defend ourselves using a variety of psychological strategies of which we may or may not be conscious or aware. Put simply, these are negative and positive coping strategies individuals use when they feel threatened. Here is a list of the major defense mechanisms and their definitions.

ACTING OUT: Behaving without awareness of the emotion behind it.
Examples: Using drugs, ditching school, running away from home.

DENIAL: Refusal to acknowledge or accept reality.
Example: Alcoholics who refuse to admit they have an alcohol problem, which allows them to continue drinking.

DISPLACEMENT: Taking out aggressive or negative feelings, thoughts, and impulses on someone else who is less threatening.
Example: A parent who had a bad day at work comes home and yells at his or her child for no reason.

HYPOCHONDRIASIS: Preoccupation with thoughts of being sick or having symptoms of illness as a way to avoid reality.
Example: An individual who constantly complains of having breathing problems related to asthma and repeatedly seeks medical appointments, medications, and treatments when there is no medical evidence of any problems with asthma.

IDEALIZATION: Perceiving someone or something to be exceptionally positive and/or ideal to avoid reality.
Example: A child brags about how "perfect" his or her mother is, when, in fact, she is an alcoholic and consistently fails to fulfill her major role obligations.

INTELLECTUALIZATION: Repeatedly approaching things from a logical or intellectual perspective, free of emotion.
Example: A scientist who only looks at the logical explanation of findings and ignores any emotional component of the process.

PROJECTION: Attributing our own negative and unacceptable feelings, thoughts, impulses, and behaviors to someone else. This enables the individual to see the faults in someone else, but also to blame the faults on the other person.

Example: Pointing out racism or sexism in someone else, when in fact, we hold racist or sexist views.

RATIONALIZATION (Justification): Explaining away or making excuses, which can lead to blaming and denials of responsibility.
Example: Making excuses for failing a drug test as if the test were faulty or contaminated or the lab made mistakes, etc.

REGRESSION: Reverting back to a younger, often childlike state.
Example: An adult having a temper tantrum.

REPRESSION: Preventing unacceptable impulses, emotions, or memories from entering conscious awareness by moving them to the subconscious.
Example: Memories of childhood trauma that may be kept in the subconscious and remembered in flashbacks.

SELF-SABOTAGE: Preventing yourself from achieving goals by doing the opposite and/or harming yourself, possibly out of a fear of failure or a fear of success.
Example: Doing something you know is wrong to avoid achieving your goal.

SUBLIMATION: Channeling negative emotions, impulses, or behaviors into positive, more acceptable ones.
Example: The individual who loves fighting and becomes a professional boxer.

Exercise

Choose the three defense mechanisms you use the most and answer the following questions. What defense mechanisms do you use the most? How often do you use these defense mechanisms (multiple times per day, daily, weekly, infrequently)? Think of situations in which you used the defense mechanisms. Were drugs involved?

What defense mechanism do you use the most?

_____

How often do you use it?

_____

In which situation have you used it?

_____
_____
_____

Were substances involved?

_____

What defense mechanism do you use the second most?

_____

How often do you use it?

_____

In which situation have you used it?

_____
_____
_____

Were substances involved?

_____

Which defense mechanism do you use the third most?

_____

How often do you use it?

_____

In which situation have you used it?

_____
_____

Were substances involved?

_____

Some defense mechanisms are common in the addiction cycle and enable the addict to continue abusing substances—namely denial, rationalization, and, of course, acting out.

EXERCISE

Denial is one defense mechanism that nearly all addicts use to maintain the picture of "normalcy," while continuing to engage in drinking or drug use. Overcoming denial and admitting you have a problem is the first step in recovery. There are many ways an addict can practice denial. For each of the questions, circle either Yes or No.

At any point in your substance abuse or addiction problem did you:

Yes   No   Deny or avoid admitting you have used substances (alcohol, drugs)?

Yes   No   Deny or avoid admitting you obtained substances?

Yes   No   Deny or avoid admitting you manufactured and/or sold drugs?

Yes   No   Deny or avoid admitting you had drug paraphernalia?

Yes   No   Deny or avoid admitting you have a substance abuse problem?

Yes   No   Deny or avoid admitting you are an addict?

Yes   No   Deny or avoid thinking about the consequences of your substance abuse or addiction?

Yes   No   Deny or avoid acknowledging the negative effects of substance abuse on your life or the lives of people around you?

Yes   No   Deny or avoid acknowledging the need for help of any kind?

Yes   No   Deny or avoid acknowledging the need for professional help (counselor, detox, treatment)?

Yes   No   Deny, avoid, or argue with others who attempted to help you?

If you answered Yes to any of these questions, you probably have struggled or currently struggle with denial. The more times you circled Yes, the more likely it is that denial has been a problem for you.

EXERCISE

Rationalization is one defense mechanism all substance abusers practice to some extent to justify the negative and harmful behaviors and minimize guilt or shame. On line A, identify rationalizations you have made with regard to your substance use, drug-seeking behaviors, or other drug-related behaviors. On line B, identify how those rationalizations hurt you or those around you.

(A) Rationalizations

(B) Effects of rationalizations on you or others

Example: (A) I'll just smoke one blunt to take the edge off.

(B) One blunt led to smoking more, and I spent the whole day smoking.

(A)_____

(B)_____

_____

(A)_____

(B)_____

_____

(A)_____

(B)_____

_____

(A)_____

(B)_____

_____

(A)_____

(B)_____

_____

(A)_____

(B)_____

_____

EXERCISE

Acting out is any negative or potentially harmful behavior that someone does, including substance abuse, drug-seeking, running away from home, committing illegal acts, or attention-seeking. In the exercise below, identify acting-out behaviors you have engaged in or continue to engage in and one negative consequence of each behavior.

ACTING-OUT BEHAVIOR	NEGATIVE CONSEQUENCE
Example: Stealing money	Mom called police and I was arrested.
_____	_____
_____	_____
_____	_____
_____	_____
_____	_____
_____	_____

Group Exercises and Discussion Topics for Defense Mechanisms

GROUP EXERCISE: ROLE PLAYS

Divide the group up into teams of two. Write down the defense mechanisms on small pieces of paper. Mix them up and have one person from each team draw from the slips of paper. Each team then role plays the defense mechanism picked. The other group members guess which defense mechanism they are depicting.

GROUP DISCUSSION

Have each group member share the three defense mechanisms they use the most, and identify which ones group members have in common. Explore how their use of defense mechanisms have positively and negatively affected their lives—and in particular, their substance use.

GROUP DISCUSSION

Have group members share their acting-out behaviors and the positive and negative ways in which these behaviors have affected their lives.

GROUP DISCUSSION

Is denial a necessary stage in the addiction process? Why and why not? Discuss.

GROUP DISCUSSION

Discuss the rationalizations people have used to justify their substance abuse and other acting-out behaviors. Do they actually believe their rationalizations at the time? If not, are they just lying to continue their behaviors, or have they convinced themselves their reasons for using are real and valid? Does denial play a role here?

GROUP EXERCISE AND DISCUSSION: MOVIE

Watch the movie *28 Days* (2000) about a woman's experience in treatment for alcoholism. Several defense mechanisms are depicted by different characters, including denial, rationalization, and acting-out. After the movie, discuss the following:

- Who appears to experience denial, and how is it depicted?

- Who rationalizes/justifies their substance abuse, and what are those rationalizations/justifications?

- Who acts out, and in what ways?

- Were there any other defense mechanisms depicted in the movie, and how were they depicted?

- What is the overall message of the movie?

———————————————

Wants vs. Needs

We often confuse wants and needs, thinking we need something that is really a want or desire. Needs are about what is necessary for basic survival and good health; they include food, water, air, and shelter. They may even include safety, security, love, and relationships. Wants are things we desire. They are not necessary for survival.

EXERCISE: IDENTIFYING NEEDS

Identify and list your needs, but be careful that what you list is an actual need, and not a want or desire. Think about what constitutes a want and what constitutes a need, and differentiate between the two. Then, write down why you need it.

NEED	WHY DO I NEED THIS?
Example: Food	Survival; I'll die without food.
_____	_____
_____	_____
_____	_____
_____	_____
_____	_____
_____	_____
_____	_____
_____	_____
_____	_____

What can you do to meet your needs?

_____

_____

EXERCISE: IDENTIFYING WANTS

Identify and list your wants, which are often, but not necessarily, things (e.g., car, vacation, item of clothing). Then, ask yourself if you have to have this want to survive or to lead a healthy life? If no, then list one thing you can do to attain that want/desire. If yes, then include it in the needs category.

WANT	ONE THING I CAN DO TO ATTAIN MY WANT/DESIRE
Example: Cell phone	Get a part-time job.
_____	_____
_____	_____
_____	_____
_____	_____
_____	_____
_____	_____
_____	_____
_____	_____

Group Exercise and Discussion Topics for Wants vs. Needs

GROUP EXERCISE

Before you begin discussing wants versus needs, have everyone in the group finish these two statements: "I want . . ." and "I need . . . ." Remember, needs are necessary for survival, whereas wants are not. Teens will often identify a want as a need, however—for example, in the case of a cell phone, because "everyone has one."

GROUP DISCUSSION

Have group members share their wants and needs and the steps they identified in meeting them. Are their wants and needs realistic? How do wants and needs change in the course of recovery?

GROUP DISCUSSION

Some people consider self-esteem and self-worth to be needs, as opposed to wants. Individuals work toward developing self-esteem and self-worth, which makes them different types of needs. Are self-esteem and self-worth necessary for happiness and fulfillment in life? Are they necessary for survival, much like food and water? Or are they merely wants? Discuss.

GROUP DISCUSSION

Is substance abuse treatment a need or a want? Is recovery from addiction a need or a want? What are the arguments for both sides? Discuss.

Impulsiveness and Consequential Thinking

Adolescents and addicts are often impulsive, meaning that they react without forethought or reflection, failing to think of the possible consequences or effects of their actions. They often *react* rather than *respond* in situations, *reacting* being more impulsive and *responding* being more reflective and thoughtful. This can lead to dangerous and potentially harmful behaviors like driving while intoxicated, stealing, or fighting. Thus, part of recovery is learning to use consequential thinking, weighing the possible consequences or effects of our actions. Addicts are often impulsive in their drug-using and drug-seeking behaviors. They seek the quick fix, resulting in behaviors like using drugs when unintended, using too much of a drug or overdosing, experimenting with other, more harmful drugs, using in more dangerous situations, or going to great lengths to get drugs—for example, through prostitution.

Keep in mind, however, that consequences can be negative or positive. There can be negative effects of using and positive effects of saying "no" to drugs. Just as negative effects can be deterrents for using, positive effects, or rewards, can help to maintain a clean and sober lifestyle.

How do we go about learning how to practice consequential thinking to reduce impulsiveness? Here are some suggestions:

- Stop. Just stop. Remind yourself to think of the effects of your possible actions. State the possible consequences out loud. Sometimes saying them out loud makes them more real. Or say them to someone for accountability.

- Stop before acting. Calm down with relaxation or breathing exercises.

- Stop and give yourself a time out, especially if you are angry and you are trying to manage your anger or reduce aggression or violence.

- Talk to someone supportive.

- Journal.

- Repeat affirmations throughout the day to remind yourself you are capable of staying clean and changing in positive ways. Write affirmations on an index card that you keep in your pocket or next to your bed. Reminding yourself you can and are changing is reaffirming.

- Talk yourself through the situation using kind gentle words to ease anxiety and reward yourself for choosing not to react impulsively.

Exercise

Complete the following statements on negative consequences:

If I relapse on alcohol or drugs, then _____ and
_____ will most likely happen.

If I lie to my family and friends about my drug use, then I take the chance of
_____ happening.

If I start experimenting with other substances, then I could _____.

If I steal from family or friends, this will probably result in_____ and
_____.

If I start skipping school, skipping work, or failing to fulfill my obligations,
_____ will most likely happen.

If I start dealing or making drugs for fast cash or to support my habit, then I could
_____ and/or _____.

EXERCISE

Complete the following statements about positive consequences:

If I reach out for help and talk to someone when I am triggered to use,
_____ and _____ may result.

If I attend a 12-Step meeting (like Alcoholics Anonymous or Narcotics Anonymous), I may
_____.

If I "come clean" with my counselor and my family about my drug abuse, then
_____ will most likely happen.

If I help myself by _____ or _____, I can
prevent myself from relapsing.

If I avoid or set boundaries with negative friends, then I may _____
or _____.

If I set goals for my future, I could _____.

Group Exercise and Discussion Topics for Impulsiveness and Consequential Thinking

GROUP EXERCISE: ROLE PLAYS

Divide the group into teams of two and three. Give them the following situations and have them strategize how they can manage these situations without reacting impulsively. Then have them play out these scenarios and their responses.

Situation 1:

You have been arguing with your parents about your curfew (you want 12:00a.m. and they want 10:00p.m.). Your first reaction is to be disrespectful and argue with them, then to leave the house angry, which increases your chance of using drugs. How can you respond instead of impulsively reacting to this situation?

Situation 2:

Your best friend lies to you and spreads a nasty rumor about you. Your first reaction is to explode on him or her, which may result in a heated argument, aggression, or drug use. How can you respond instead of impulsively reacting to the situation?

Situation 3:

You are hanging out with friends on a lazy Saturday afternoon. One of your friends says he brought some "mary jane" (marijuana) and asks you if you want to smoke some. Your friends are pressuring you to "take a hit." How can you use consequential thinking and avoid reacting by smoking the weed or worse?

Situation 4:

You go into a store with two of your friends and, without telling you beforehand, they grab some alcohol and run out of the store. Do you react by running with them? How do you manage this situation without reacting on impulse?

GROUP EXERCISE

Have group members write affirmations or friendly, positive reminders on index cards that they can read through daily. Have them share these affirmations out loud. These affirmations or positive statements can encourage them to remain clean and sober and not to give in to temptations. Or, they can be reminders of what could happen if they don't take care of themselves.

GROUP DISCUSSION

Discuss how impulsiveness has contributed to school problems (e.g., impulsively cutting class, getting into fights, using on campus, stealing). Sometimes impulsiveness is related to or due to ADHD, which usually becomes apparent through school problems at an early age. Discuss how impulsiveness has affected your education and your overall goal of graduating.

GROUP DISCUSSION

Discuss how impulsiveness has contributed to legal problems. What illegal acts were committed as a result of reacting impulsively (e.g., theft, carjacking, assault)? Has anyone in the group been cited for misdemeanors, arrested, placed in juvenile hall, or placed on probation? How has this, in turn, affected substance abuse?

GROUP DISCUSSION

Discuss how impulsiveness has contributed to problems at home or within the family. Has trust and honesty been broken? Has impulsiveness led to running away from home or "going on the run?" How has impulsiveness and lack of consequential thinking impacted relationships with parents and other family members?

GROUP DISCUSSION: SELF-LIMITING BEHAVIORS

Self-limiting behaviors are old, negative behaviors that are often impulsive and may ultimately limit an individual's potential to remain clean and sober. These behaviors may be destructive and harmful to ourselves and others emotionally or physically, and may limit our ability to develop and practice healthier, more adaptive behaviors. Examples include lying, cheating, stealing, drug use, and self-sabotage. Have each group member identify five self-limiting behaviors they struggle with and, as a group, discuss how these may prevent them from living clean and sober. Strategize and explore, as a group, how members can change, reduce, or stop their self-limiting behaviors.

Feelings, Attitudes, and Behaviors in Interaction

Often when acting impulsively, there is little or no consideration of feelings or attitudes. In reality, feelings, attitudes, and behaviors are closely linked; each aspect of the triad causes and affects the other aspects as diagrammed below. Behaviors cause and affect feelings and attitudes; feelings cause and affect attitudes and behaviors; and attitudes cause and affect feelings and behaviors.

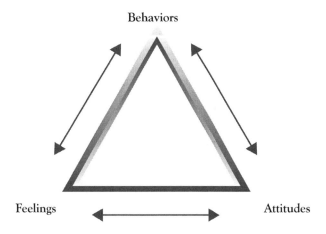

EXCERCISE

In the diagrams below, list the possible feelings and attitudes that may cause and affect the given behaviors.

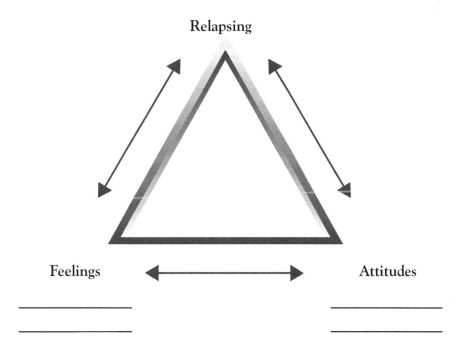

Lying to Friends and Family About Drug Use

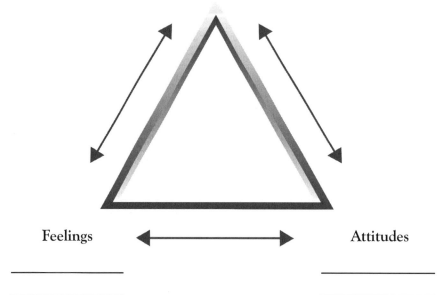

Feelings   Attitudes

_____   _____

_____   _____

Choosing Not to Use When Given the Choice and Asked

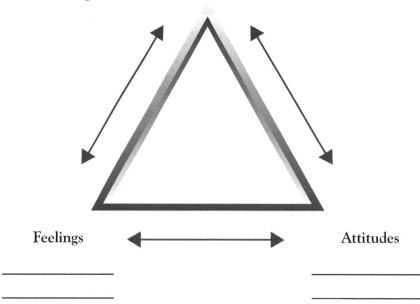

Feelings   Attitudes

_____   _____

_____   _____

Now list the possible attitudes and behaviors when given the feeling.

Behaviors

_____

_____

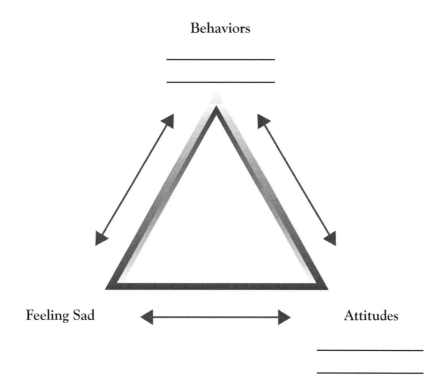

Feeling Sad ←——————————→ Attitudes

_____

_____

Behaviors

_____

_____

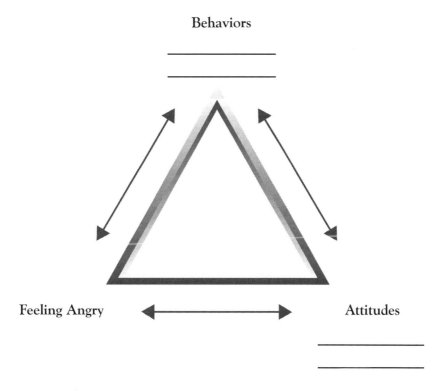

Feeling Angry ←——————————→ Attitudes

_____

_____

Finally, list the possible feelings and behaviors when given the attitude.

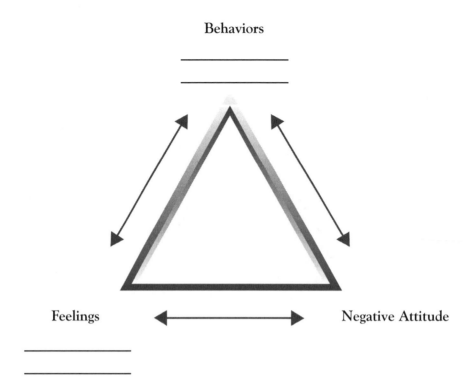

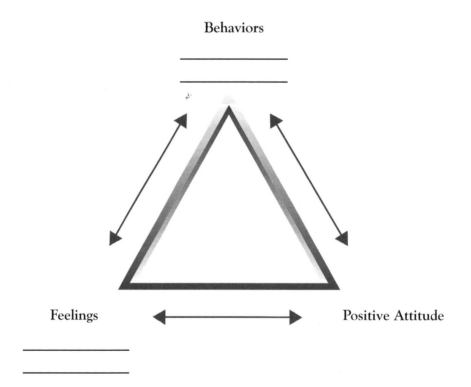

Group Exercise and Discussion Topics for Feelings, Attitudes, and Behaviors in Interaction

GROUP DISCUSSION

How do consequences fit into the interactions between feelings, thoughts, and behaviors? How can understanding these interactions better enable someone to practice consequential thinking?

GROUP DISCUSSION

Identifying and experiencing feelings can be a challenge in the process of recovery. Sometimes individuals use substances to avoid feeling hurt or angry. Discuss the different feelings with which group members struggle and explore ways of coping with uncomfortable feelings.

GROUP EXERCISE AND DISCUSSION

On a board, have each group member draw two triangles—a maladaptive triangle with relapse as the primary behavior, and an adaptive/helpful triangle in response to relapse. Compare and contrast the negative and positive triangles. How can group members help one another? Discuss.

5

Understanding How
Relationships Affect Substance Use

Family Tree: Genetics and Substance Use

Substance abuse and addiction are usually the result of nature (genetics) and nurture (environment). Often, we don't realize how much family affects the development of a substance abuse problem/addiction until we see a genogram (family tree). In the following exercise and using the guide, trace your family tree one step at a time and take notice of redundant patterns, transitions, or traumas that are passed from one generation to another.

Example:

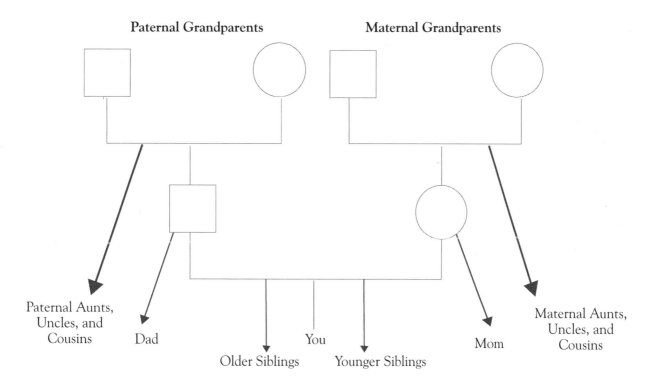

Symbols and Format:

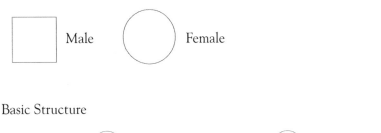

Male   Female

Basic Structure

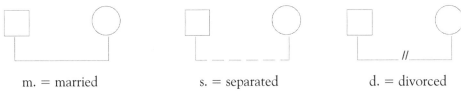

m. = married   s. = separated   d. = divorced

b. = born (include year)   ∧ = Signifies twins

X = deceased   { } = Signifies adopted individual

o = Signifies pregnancy

Additional Optional Information:
e. = ethnicity
r. = race
a. = religious affiliation

Patterns of interactions and relationships:
======= Close relationship
∧∧∧∧∧ = Conflictual relationship
∧∧∧∧∧ = Passive/aggressive, or close and conflictual relationship

Drawing the Family Tree

1. Identify your parents. Include names, ages, and whether your parents are married, divorced, or separated.

2. Identify yourself. Include your name and age.

3. Identify your siblings, oldest to youngest (left to right), and whether they have the same parents as you or one common parent. Include their names and ages. Include step-parents (if any).

4. Identify your grandparents. Include names and ages. If they are deceased, note this by putting an X through the square or circle.

5. Identify aunts and uncles (parental siblings). Include names and ages. Then identify their spouses/partners and their children (your cousins). Include names and ages.

6. Identify nieces and nephews (if any), and include names and ages.

7. If you want, you can identify ethnicity, race, or religion of family members. Also, you can continue to draw fourth and fifth generations if you so choose.

8. Identify interactions or relationship patterns (very close, conflictual, or passive-aggressive).

Now, looking at the family tree, identify the following using colors. Either color in the square or circle or write in the specific color.

1. Use *red* to identify everyone who has/had a substance abuse problem or addiction, and identify his/her drug of choice (including alcohol and nicotine).

2. Use *yellow* to identify who has/had a mental health problem or psychiatric disorder like depression, bipolar disorder, anxiety disorder, PTSD, developmental disorder (e.g., autism), psychotic disorder, schizophrenia, dementia, Alzheimer's, etc.

3. Use *green* to identify who has/had a medical health problem like heart disease, heart attack, stroke, cardiovascular disease, cancer, etc.

4. Use *blue* to identify who has been traumatized by physical, sexual, or emotional abuse, domestic violence, neglect, rape, kidnapping, etc. Identify the perpetrator of the crime if within the family.

You can also identify who has/had problems with the law and/or been imprisoned using *orange*; use *purple* to identify who is/was in the military.

MY FAMILY TREE

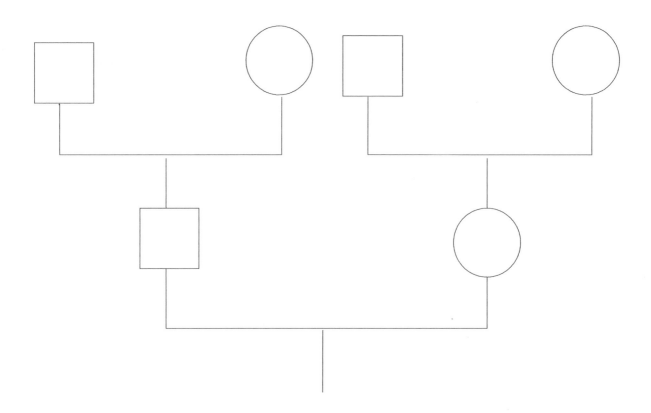

Learning from the Family Tree

Answer the following questions as best you can, since you may not have any details. What is most important is identifying patterns in your family.

1. Who has/had substance abuse or addiction problems, and what are their drugs of choice? Do you know if any of them have been in treatment (at a hospital, detox facility, residential or outpatient program) and are they in recovery? Could any of those who are clean and sober be a support to you?

   _____

   _____

   _____

   _____

   _____

2. Who has/had a mental health or psychiatric condition, and if so, what? Is/was it a short-term and acute or long-term and chronic condition? Were they treated with medications? Do you notice any patterns in mental health?

   _____

   _____

   _____

   _____

   _____

3. Who has/had a medical problem or condition, and did it leave them disabled? Have they taken medication for this condition? Do you notice any patterns in or between the generations (for example, do multiple people have cancer or heart conditions)? Are any of their medical conditions related to their substance abuse (for example, did they contract hepatitis from dirty needles or HIV from unprotected sex while drunk or high)?

   _____

   _____

   _____

   _____

   _____

4. Do any of those with substance abuse or addiction problems also have either mental health or medical conditions or both? (If so, they would have dual diagnoses. This is very common among addicts.)

_____

_____

_____

_____

_____

5. Who is/was the victim of a trauma, most notably the victim of physical, sexual, or emotional abuse or neglect? Who is/was the perpetrator and was the perpetrator also a victim? Was the perpetrator(s) charged with any crime? Notice if any of the substance abusers or addicts also had a history of trauma. Substance abuse or addiction may have served as a means of coping with the trauma.

_____

_____

_____

_____

_____

6. What are the patterns of interactions/relationships you notice? Are there any very close relationships? Could they be enmeshed (so close that the relationship is harmful)? Are there any conflictual relationships? Are there any passive-aggressive relationships? Have any of these patterns impacted you and your substance abuse or addiction?

_____

_____

_____

_____

_____

7. Is there anyone else you would like to include in your family tree who is not a biological relative (e.g., nanny, caretaker, foster child or foster parent, neighbor)? Can they be a source of support to you?

_____

_____

_____

_____

_____

Group Exercise and Discussion Topics for Genetics and Substance Use

GROUP EXERCISE

Give group members the option of completing their family trees on a poster board to enhance their importance. They may find it is easier to include all the labels on a larger surface that they can share with their families. Offer them an assortment of art supplies to draw their family trees. Then, after everyone has completed their tree and answered the questions, give the group members an opportunity to share the trees and what they learned from the exercise with the other group members.

GROUP DISCUSSION

Are there any patterns that are common among group members (for example, patterns of addiction or illness that are present among generations)? Discuss how these patterns have affected the group members themselves and if these patterns have contributed to the development and/or maintenance of their substance abuse problems?

GROUP DISCUSSION

Discuss the concept of dysfunctional vs. "normal" families. How many group members label their families dysfunctional, and what distinguishes a dysfunctional family from a "normal" family? Is there such a thing as a normal family?

GROUP DISCUSSION

How many group members are children of alcoholics and/or drug addicts? Discuss how parental substance abuse affected them and their own substance abuse problems. How can they break the cycle of addiction? Did parental substance abuse affect relationship patterns? Was there a lot of conflict in the home? How has this affected their relationship patterns?

Children of Alcoholics/Addicts

Alcoholism—and addiction in general—is a family problem in that it affects everyone in the immediate family, not just the alcoholic or addict. Households with an alcoholic (or drug-addicted) parent experience life differently, as there tends to be more overall dysfunction, increased conflict, less family cohesion, and less communication in the home, as well as higher rates of domestic violence, child abuse, neglect, and aggression in general (NACOA, 2012).

Children of alcoholic (or drug-using) parents (COAs) are at increased risk for developing mental health problems like depression and anxiety disorders. These mental health problems may serve as a means of protection and adaptation from low self-esteem and low self-worth, which is common in COAs. They often struggle with feelings of shame, embarrassment, guilt, and self-blame, which reinforce the low self-esteem and low self-worth—shame and embarrassment about their alcoholic or addicted parents, their parents' behaviors, and their environment at home; guilt about their parents' behaviors and their inability to stop them from drinking (or using drugs); and self-blame, as they often feel responsible for their parents' drinking or (drug use) (NACOA, 2012; Sher, 1997). The guilt and self-blame gives COAs a false sense of control over their parents' alcoholism (or drug addiction). They may also become "parentified" as they play the parent and care for their siblings.

COAs are also more at risk for developing educational or school-related problems. They are at greater risk for developing learning problems like poor cognitive (thinking) abilities, poor abstract thinking, and poor problem-solving abilities (NACOA, 2012). They may demonstrate school problems like truancy, suspensions, and expulsions, and are at increased risk for failing classes, flunking, refusing to get along with teachers or authority figures, and dropping out of school (NACOA, 2012).

Infants born to mothers who drank while pregnant are at greater risk for developing Fetal Alcohol Syndrome and subsequent developmental disabilities, affecting all aspects of life. Does any of this seem familiar?

Exercise

Answer the following questions if this pertains to you or your home situation:

1. Are you the child of a parent who is an alcoholic or problem drinker (drug user/addict)? Was it your mother or father, or both, or a step-parent? Are you or any of your siblings problem drinkers or alcoholics (or drug users/addicts)? Do you think there is a connection?

_____

_____

_____

_____

_____

2. Was there a non-alcoholic (or non-drug-using) parent in the household, and how did he or she react to the alcoholic (or drug-using) parent? Did that parent try to compensate for the alcoholic (or drug-using) parent? Or did he or she enable the alcoholic (or addict) by behaving in ways that supported or increased the drinking (or drug use)?

_____

_____

_____

_____

_____

3. Was there a lot of conflict, either verbal arguing or physical fighting, in the household, and how often did it happen (daily, weekly, monthly)? What was that like for you, and how did the conflict affect you?

_____

_____

_____

_____

_____

Was the conflict often about the alcoholic parent's drinking (or drug use)? Do any conflicts stand out for you, or were you particularly affected by a specific incident? What happened, and how did it affect you?

_____

_____

_____

_____

_____

4. Did the police or CPS ever step in and come to the house? What happened and what was that like for you?

_____

_____

_____

_____

_____

5. Did your parent ever get stopped or arrested for drinking while driving or driving under the influence? What was the result?

_____

_____

_____

_____

_____

6. Did you ever plead with your alcoholic (or drug-using) parent to stop drinking (or using)? What was his or her response?

_____

_____

_____

_____

_____

7. Did you ever feel or experience shame or embarrassment about your parent's drinking (or drug use) or your situation at home? How has this affected you?

_____

_____

_____

_____

_____

8. Did you ever feel guilty or blame yourself for your parent's drinking (even though in no way, shape, or form was it your fault, and there was nothing you could have done to stop it)? How has this affected you?

_____

_____

_____

_____

_____

9. Do you struggle with depression, mood swings, or anxiety problems? How has this affected your life? Do you think you drink or use substances to cope with these negative feelings or to avoid them?

_____

_____

_____

_____

_____

10. How has your upbringing affected who you are today and how you relate to people? How do you define the concept of family, and has your upbringing affected how you think of family?

_____

_____

_____

_____

_____

11. Do you want something different for your own children some day? How can you stop this cycle of addiction in your family?

_____

_____

_____

_____

_____

Group Discussion Topics for Children of Alcoholics/Addicts

GROUP DISCUSSION

Children of alcoholics or addicts (COAs) are at higher risk for neglect, abuse, and abandonment as their parent's addiction progresses. This can lead to issues with insecurity, attachment, trust, and emotional problems. How could this affect their ability to form close relationships with others? How can they overcome this? Can anyone in the group relate?

Group Discussion

COAs often become "parentified"—meaning that they assume the role of mother or father in the home—especially if they have younger siblings. For example, they may help raise their siblings, cook, clean, and run errands as a parent would typically do. Can anyone in the group relate and/or is this the actual scenario at home for anyone? How might this situation motivate or deter someone from using substances? How might someone positively or negatively cope in the parentified role? How can this affect relationships? Discuss.

Group Discussion

Some COAs may experience shame and/or embarrassment growing up. They may be ashamed of or embarrassed by their family, the state of the house, or their alcoholic/drug-using parent's behaviors. This shame can affect how COAs think of themselves, lowering self-esteem, self-confidence, and self-worth. Can anyone in the group relate? How can the group help them cope? Discuss.

Group Discussion

COAs may feel guilty about their parents' drinking or drug use, thinking they are causing the parent to drink or use drugs, especially at younger ages when children are more egocentric. They may have the false notion that, if they were better, smarter, or somehow different, their parent would stop drinking. Ask the group if anyone can relate to this—if they have experienced, in the past or present, guilt around parental substance abuse. How has this affected their ability to cope? How has this affected their own substance use? (Help the group to understand that their parents' substance abuse is not caused by anything they have done or said—that their parents do so regardless of their children.

Enabling Behaviors

Enabling refers to the act of allowing an alcoholic/addict to continue using their substances without consequences. Family members are usually the most prone to enabling. While they have good intentions and see themselves as being helpful, in reality they are hurting the alcoholic or addict because this keeps them in the cycle of addiction. For example, the classic enabling scenario is when an alcoholic husband's wife calls in to his job and says he won't be in today because he has the flu when, in reality, he is hung-over. Other enabling behaviors include cleaning up after alcoholics or addicts, making excuses for them, bailing them out of jail, or paying their bills, tickets, fines, etc. Furthermore, we may be enabling others like parents to continue their addictive behaviors; in so doing, we may assume the mother or father role. Addiction, after all, is really a family problem.

Part of recovery involves identifying enabling behaviors and counter-acting them by not doing them! For example, your parents may enable your use by calling school and telling the attendance person that you won't be in school today because you are sick when, in reality, you're "coming down" off drugs. The best treatment is to let alcoholics or addicts deal with their own consequences, not to prevent the consequences.

EXERCISE

Answer the following questions:

1. Who in your family, including yourself, is an alcoholic or addict? Who "benefits" from enabling in your family? _____
   Who is an enabler? _____

2. What are some enabling behaviors family or friends engage in that keep you in the cycle of substance abuse?

   _____
   _____

3. How do these enabling behaviors keep you using?

   _____
   _____

4. What can family or friends do to stop the enabling?

   _____
   _____

First, write down enabling behaviors in which you or someone close to you engage that allow sub-stance abuse to continue. You may be enabling someone else, and/or someone else may be enabling you. Second, identify who engages in these enabling behaviors—you, a parent, a sibling, a friend, or a significant other. Finally, identify the alcoholic or addict, the person most likely benefitting from these behaviors. You may find that enabling is common in your family or circle of friends.

ENABLING BEHAVIOR	WHO ENABLES (THE ENABLER)	WHO IS BEING ENABLED (THE ADDICT)
Example: Giving money for drugs	Mom and Dad	Me
Example: Doing mom's chores around the house when she's hung over	Me	Mom

Group Exercise and Discussion Topics for Enabling Behaviors

GROUP DISCUSSION

Often in an alcoholic household, the sober parent engages in enabling behaviors like cleaning up after the alcoholic, calling work and making excuses for why the alcoholic parent can't work, fulfilling responsibilities of the alcoholic parent, even buying the alcohol. The sober parent often tries to compensate for the alcoholic parent, especially if there are children involved. The enabler does not necessarily need to be the spouse; children, grandparents, or other relatives can be enablers as well. Ask the group members to identify the enablers in their families, if there is/was one—and most likely there is/was. What kind of enabling behaviors did they engage in? How did this affect the children/group members? Did it ultimately increase or decrease the alcoholic's drinking?

GROUP DISCUSSION

What fuels enabling? Sometimes it's the enabler's own codependency issues and his or her underlying insecurities. Codependency occurs when someone is overly invested emotionally in other people, trying constantly to make others happy and "fix" their problems, because it is only when others are happy that the codependent can be happy. If addicts are sad or angry, however, their codependents feel driven to "fix" whatever is wrong to make them happy—for example, paying the addicts' debts or bail, cleaning up after them, or buying them alcohol. In the long run, this fuels the addiction. Have group members discuss who the codependents are in their families. How has the codependency and enabling affected the family? How has it affected their substance use?

GROUP DISCUSSION

Discuss how enabling affects substance abuse/addiction. In what ways does enabling "benefit" and "hurt" the substance abuser/addict? In what ways does enabling "benefit" and "hurt" the enabler? How does enabling affect others in the family, and does it change their roles in the family?

GROUP EXERCISE: HOMEWORK ASSIGNMENT

Have all individuals in the group have a discussion with someone in their families whom they identify as an enabler—either alone, as a family, or, preferably, in family therapy. (Keep in mind that the enablers probably aren't even aware they are enabling.) Ask group members to define enabling and list the ways in which they've been enabled. Also, explore how the enabling has actually increased or worsened the substance abuse. Then, explore ways in which the enablers can stop enabling and help the addicts to decrease their use. In the next group, have individuals discuss what it was like to talk about enabling with the enablers, and process any leftover thoughts or feelings.

Positive and Negative Relationships

Relationships can be characterized in many different ways—as "blood" (genetic) or family, as partnerships that may or may not be intimate, as friendships, and as acquaintances. There is also a difference between relationships in the home, in the family, in places of employment, in the community, and within ourselves. Moreover, relationships can be distinguished as positive or negative. Positive relationships are healthy; negative relationships are not.

EXERCISE

Take a moment to identify what makes a relationship positive. Is it defined by honesty, openness, or love? Then identify what makes a relationship negative. Is it characterized by using substances, engaging in criminal activities, or covering up for one another?

CHARACTERISTICS OF POSITIVE RELATIONSHIPS	CHARACTERISTICS OF NEGATIVE RELATIONSHIPS
Honesty	Dishonesty
Trustworthiness	Drug Use
Accountability	Agression

EXERCISE

List all those persons whom you believe are positive influences (positive relationships) and negative influences (negative relationships) in your life. Be as specific and as honest as possible. You may realize that some of your "closest" relationships are actually negative influences in your life, and you may need to set some boundaries with them or avoid them altogether in order to prevent relapse.

POSITIVE PEERS / RELATIONSHIPS	NEGATIVE PEERS / RELATIONSHIPS

Ask yourself these questions: How can I "deal with" negative relationships in my life: by avoiding negative people, by setting boundaries with them, or both? What strategies can I use to avoid negative people? What strategies can I use to set boundaries with negative people?

_____

_____

_____

_____

_____

EXERCISE: SUPPORT NETWORK

What is a support network? A group of individuals you choose from your list of positive relationships who will help you through the hard times, bring you positive energy, and enable you to remain clean and sober. Identify those supportive people, write down their phone numbers and email addresses, and put them where you can reach them in a time of crisis or every day.

SUPPORTIVE PERSON	PHONE NUMBER	EMAIL ADDRESS
_____	_____	_____
_____	_____	_____
_____	_____	_____
_____	_____	_____
_____	_____	_____

Group Exercise and Discussion Topics for Positive and Negative Relationships

GROUP EXERCISE AND DISCUSSION: SETTING BOUNDARIES WITH NEGATIVE FRIENDS

Some individuals in recovery may choose to avoid or no longer associate with negative friends (those who use substances), which is usually the best strategy. Still others may choose to continue associating and socializing with negative friends, but set boundaries around substances and substance use—for example, setting firm limits by telling them not to bring alcohol or drugs around you. In this exercise, have two people role play the following situations in which they practice setting boundaries with negative people. Discuss the role plays afterward—in particular, what made setting boundaries difficult or challenging.

Situation 1—Phone conversation:
One of your best friends, who smokes pot daily, calls you up after you've been clean for awhile and asks if you want to go hang out. You know this person is still using. Do you hang up on this friend? Do you cut the conversation short and tell him or her not to call you again? Do you talk for awhile and tell the person you no longer can hang out if he or she uses? How do you set boundaries with this friend?

Situation 2—Conversation with a group of friends:
Several of your friends are hanging out in the neighborhood, smoking pot and drinking alcohol. They see you walking down the street and call out to you, offering you some pot and alcohol. How do you set boundaries with a group of negative friends who are using?

Situation 3—Setting boundaries with a family member:
You are home with your sister (or brother or other close family member), and you know she (or he) uses on a regular basis, smoking weed, drinking alcohol, and possibly taking pills. Your parents aren't home. How do you go about setting limits with her (or him), and what kind of limits do you set?

GROUP DISCUSSION

Discuss as a group what characterizes negative vs. positive relationships and who may fall into each category. Then explore how group members can go about making new, positive relationships.

GROUP DISCUSSION

Some adolescents struggle with anyone in a position of authority—teachers, police officers, probation officers, or even parents. Discuss how authority figures may help group members and how they may be part of your positive support network.

Managing Peer Pressure

Peer pressure occurs when peers, usually of a similar age, try to influence you to behave, think, or feel a certain way. Sometimes you may behave in a way you had not originally intended because of this pressure to conform with, please, or satisfy others. For example, teens often start experimenting with drugs as a result of the undue influence of peers because of a fear of not being accepted or of being criticized by others.

EXERCISE

Answer the following questions:

1. What role did peer pressure play in your experimenting with or using drugs? What was that experience like at the time? What did you feel then? What do you think now that you are looking back on it?

_____

_____

_____

_____

_____

2. Did peer pressure lead to continued substance use? How?

_____

_____

_____

_____

_____

3. Did peer pressure lead to stealing (to buy drugs), selling drugs, or even making drugs? How?

_____

_____

_____

_____

_____

4. What role did curiosity play in experimenting with drugs?

_____

_____

_____

_____

_____

5. What role did early childhood exposure to drugs play? Was there family peer pressure to experiment with or use drugs? If so, what was that like, and how do you feel about it now?

_____

_____

_____

_____

_____

6. What do you think would have resulted if you had not given in to peer pressure? Loss of friends? Embarrassment? Violence? Some other result?

_____

_____

_____

_____

_____

7. Looking back, what was worse: giving in and using, or fighting the peer pressure?

_____

_____

_____

_____

_____

EXERCISE

Here is a set of possible coping strategies. Check which strategies may have been useful in dealing with the situations previously discussed, and which strategies you are willing and able to use in the future.

In Past Situations	In Future Situations	
____	____	Leave the situation
____	____	Make an excuse
____	____	Set boundaries by . . .
____	____	. . . telling peers not to drink or use drugs around you (or you will leave, not hang with them)
____	____	. . . telling peers not to bring alcohol or drugs around you
____	____	. . . telling peers not to come to your house
____	____	. . . telling peers not to call or contact you
____	____	Have an "escape" plan
____	____	Attend activities with someone who is clean and sober
____	____	Have the phone number of a clean and sober person on whom you can call in an emergency
____	____	Plan to go to an NA or AA meeting later
____	____	Engage in other distracting activities at the time
____	____	Tell peers you can't use substances because . . .
____	____	. . . you are in recovery
____	____	. . . you get drug tested regularly
____	____	. . . using would violate probation

__	__	. . . someone at home called saying there was an emergency, and you must leave
__	__	. . . you have a test at school the next day, early
__	__	. . . you have to work the next day, early
__	__	. . . you're sick
__	__	. . . probation set a curfew for you and you can't stay

Group Exercises and Discussion Topics for Managing Peer Pressure

GROUP EXERCISE: ROLE PLAYS TO MANAGE PEER PRESSURE

Divide the group into groups of two and three. Copy these role plays onto separate sheets of paper, fold them up, and have one group member from each team pick a role play out of a bowl. Then have the groups act out the role play they chose about how to manage peer pressure, strategizing and coming up with some ways to manage the peer pressure and not to drink or use drugs.

Scenario 1:
You've been clean for three months. One night, you are hanging out with friends and one takes out a bag of weed, offering it to you. You struggle with wanting and not wanting to smoke it. Do you take one big hit "for old time's sake"? Do you stay in that situation or do you leave? How can you get out of the situation? Do you tell your parents? What about your counselor?

Scenario 2:
You are at a party and friends are drinking beer, which they offer to you. What do you do? What are two excuses you can use to avoid drinking? How will you leave the situation? Do you stay at the party or go?

Scenario 3:
You are standing outside of a store with a friend. He or she asks if you want to go in and grab some Coricidin or cough syrup and run out so that you two can go home and "get high." Your friend is pressuring you to steal it. What do you do? Do you explore the possible consequences? Do you talk your friend out of it or go along with it?

Scenario 4:

You are hanging out with a group of friends who are smoking spice. They ask you if you want any, and you say no. But they start pressuring you to try it, saying: "Come on, try it, you'll love it. Don't be square." Do you give in to the peer pressure to experiment with spice, or do you turn them down? Do you tell them "no" and not to ask you or bring it around you again?

Scenario 5:

You are walking to the 7/11 with a few friends to get sodas and snacks. You see your dealer hanging out at the corner and he doesn't know you've been clean for six months. Your friends try to convince you to go buy some drugs from the dealer. One of your friends says: "Hey, let's go score some dope and crank up the party!" Do you ignore your friends? Do you ignore the dealer? How do you manage the situation?

GROUP DISCUSSION

What are some of the strategies groups came up with in the situations they role played in the above exercise? Did they leave the situation? Set boundaries with peers? Make excuses not to use? Engage in some other form of distraction?

GROUP DISCUSSION

What role did peer pressure play in experimenting with and using drugs? What role did curiosity play? Have the group members explore how pressure from peers to experiment with substances changed their lives. If it weren't for peer pressure, how many group members would probably not have experimented with or used drugs? What does this say about peer pressure in general?

GROUP DISCUSSION

Is lying ever a plausible strategy? Are there any "good" or "bad" lies, if it means your recovery?

GROUP EXERCISE AND DISCUSSION: MOVIE

Have the group watch the movie *Some Kind of Wonderful* (1995). Discuss the following:

- What role did peer pressure play in the movie?
- Who experienced peer pressure, and how did they respond?
- What relationships were negative? What relationships were positive?
- To which character did each group member relate and why?
- In what ways was peer pressure good or bad?

Media Influences

Media—television, movies, music, magazines, newspapers, video games, the Internet—can have an impact on how individuals think about substance abuse. Some messages that promote substance abuse may be subtle, others very obvious. Think of the multiple messages we get every day from the media about substance use and abstinence, and how this may influence adolescents' decisions to use or not to use substances. Moreover, the media can influence how individuals think about themselves and others, having a positive or negative influence on self-esteem, self-image, and self-identity. How does the media influence what adolescents do and think and how they behave? How does this affect self-image and self-esteem? And how does this affect adolescent substance abuse?

EXERCISE

Answer the following questions:

1. How much time do you spend each day listening to or watching forms of media (watching TV or movies, listening to music, playing video games, surfing the web, reading magazines or newspapers)?

   _____

   _____

2. Do some media forms promote substance use (of any kind)? Do some movies promote substance use (you can list specific movies if you want to)? How do they promote it?

   _____

   What about television?

   _____

   What about music like rap, hard rock, or underground?

   _____

   What about video games or on-line games?

   _____

   What about magazines or newspapers?

   _____

   What about the Internet?

   _____

3. Does the media promote substance abstinence? If so, how?

_____

_____

_____

4. Does the media promote violence? If so, how?

_____

_____

_____

5. How does the media treat males and females? What are the subtle or blatant messages the media gives you about the sexes? Is there a gender bias? If so, how is that communicated?

_____

_____

_____

6. How does the media treat different cultures, ethnicities, or races? Is there a bias for or against any of these groups? What is the message, and how is this communicated?

_____

_____

_____

7. Does the media promote any specific body type? Is there a perfect body image? How is this communicated?

_____

_____

_____

8. How has the media affected your self-image—how you think about yourself and your body?

_____

_____

_____

9. As a result, do you have a positive or negative view about yourself as a person? Do you have a positive or negative view about your body?

_____

_____

_____

10. How has this view of yourself affected your substance abuse? What about your behaviors? Your lifestyle in general?

_____

_____

_____

Group Exercises and Discussion Topics for Media Influences

GROUP EXERCISE AND DISCUSSION

Divide the group into teams of between three and five people. Give them ten minutes to look through a stack of magazines for ads, articles, or pictures promoting substance use (alcohol, drugs, cigarettes). Tear the ads out. Then give the groups ten minutes to look for ads, articles, or pictures promoting abstinence. Afterward, count the number promoting alcohol and drugs vs. the number promoting abstinence. Are there more articles promoting substance use? Discuss as a group what this says about the impact of the media on adolescent drug use?

GROUP EXERCISE

Rap or music in general influences adolescents. Have the group write a rap or a song about abstinence from drugs and alcohol. If the group is too big, divide them into two separate groups and have them perform the resulting songs in front of each other. The group(s) may choose to videotape or record the song(s) so that they can watch them again.

GROUP DISCUSSION

Discuss how music in today's world influences adolescents to use substances. Consider all the musicians who sing or rap about drugs, sex, and violence. What are the subtle or blatant messages they are sending, and how does it ultimately influence young people? Why?

Pick any of the forms of media listed and discuss how that media form influences adolescents' self-esteem and self-image—how they view themselves in the world as individuals, internally and externally. How has the media positively and negatively influenced their self-esteem and self-image? Low self-esteem or negative body image can lead some people to use drugs as an escape from feelings or reality. Discuss this connection and how it relates to group members.

———————————————————

6

Building Communication Skills

Honest Communication Part I—Honesty

Improving and enhancing honest communication is necessary in the recovery process. Addiction and substance abuse can impair what was once good communication and lead adolescents to decrease communication and be more dishonest. Honest communication has two parts. One essential aspect is honesty (telling the truth), but so often, as the substance abuse worsens, the ability to be honest suffers. The substance abuser tells one lie ("No, I didn't use"), which often leads to other lies to cover up the original lie, causing a snowball effect of lies.

Part of recovery involves "coming clean," accounting for our dishonesty and negative behaviors, taking responsibility for both, and compensating for them (righting the wrongs). Taking responsibility means admitting our wrongs and not blaming anyone or anything else for our behaviors. An honest apology is often enough to right the wrongs. Sometimes, however, we may need to pay a consequence to make things right—for example, paying a fine or restitution if we break laws. Regardless, being honest about our mistakes is the first step in developing positive and open communication.

EXERCISE

To begin practicing honest communication, answer the following questions about your own honesty and dishonesty:

1. What have I been dishonest about and/or lied about, and to whom?

_____

_____

_____

2. Have I "come clean" about my dishonesty? Have I acknowledged and taken responsibility for lies I have told, and to the appropriate persons?

_____
_____
_____

3. What have I done to correct these wrongs?

_____
_____
_____

4. Not all lies have to be big lies. We may tell numerous "little white lies," thinking they are harmless and unimportant. But the little lies add up too. Account for the little lies by filling in the blanks.

Examples: I told my parents I didn't know what happened to the missing liquor, when I actually drank it *or* I lied to my parents about not using meth.

I told (person)(the lie I told)_____

I told _____

I told _____

I told _____

I was dishonest to (person)(about)_____

I was dishonest to _____

I was dishonest to _____

I was dishonest to _____

I lied to (person)(about)_____

I lied to _____

I lied to _____

I lied to _____

5. How do you feel after acknowledging all these big lies and those "little white lies"? Do you feel a sense of relief?

_____

_____

_____

_____

Group Exercises and Discussion Topics for Honesty

GROUP EXERCISE AND DISCUSSION

Have everyone in the group write down on a note card anonymously one lie or dishonest thing they said while using substances or about their substance abuse. Have everyone fold the cards in half and return them to the group leader. The leader then picks out one card at a time to read aloud and discuss with the group. Remember, the statements on the cards are anonymous. Chances are other group members may relate and discuss their own experiences. Discuss the different responses people give. Can others relate?

GROUP EXERCISE

Part of recovery, as explored in the 12 Steps, is to make a list of the ways in which you have hurt (or lied to) other people, to acknowledge these wrongs, and to make amends to the people you have hurt. This includes identifying and acknowledging the lies you have told. For some, making amends simply means apologizing; for others, it may mean compensating in some way—replacing something or making restitution, for example. Have group members identify some of these wrongs and strategize how to go about making amends. Role play these situations.

GROUP DISCUSSION

Discuss the concept of the snowball effect as it pertains to dishonesty (covering up one lie with another and another until it becomes a big ball of lies). How has that played out in the lives of group members? Once you get stuck in the cycle, how can you get out?

GROUP DISCUSSION

Dishonesty can be a learned behavior if we have witnessed parents or loved ones being dishonest. On the other hand, it can be a method of self-preservation and protection. Maybe it's both. What do group members think about this? Do they think it's a learned behavior, or a choice?

GROUP DISCUSSION

Is there ever a justification for lying? Does it depend on the situation (e.g., if someone could be hurt if you tell them the truth)? Or is it wrong to lie, regardless of the situation or consequences? Discuss group members' thoughts on this.

———————————————

Honest Communication Part II—Communication Skills

The second part of honest communication is learning and practicing effective communication skills, which include:

- Engaging in active listening
- Using "I" statements
- Speaking clearly and staying on topic
- Avoiding name-calling
- Avoiding all-or-nothing statements
- Avoiding swearing
- Making eye contact
- Using appropriate body language

The most important aspect of effective communication is active listening. This is different from hearing, which is the mechanics of processing sound that enters the ears. We do this automatically. In contrast, listening involves hearing, plus taking in what someone says and processing the message without reacting or giving feedback right away. It means processing or thinking about what the other person says and reflecting it back to them (summarizing what you hear).

The second aspect of effective communication is using "I" statements, or speaking in the first person—making comments like "I feel…." Speaking in the first person—not making comments that start with "You…"—reduces blame and subsequent defensive reactions. For example, saying "I feel angry when you…" is more effective than saying "You make me angry when you…," because the speaker takes ownership of his or her feelings and is less likely to cause an argument.

Speaking clearly and staying on topic without switching subjects or introducing irrelevant topics makes communication more effective. Be specific in what you say, and speak with clarity. Mumbling only complicates things and may lead to frustration. Furthermore, don't skip from topic to topic. Rather, discuss one subject at a time, which reduces confusion.

When discussing a topic, always avoid name-calling, labeling, and making any kind of racist, sexist, homophobic, or other derogatory comments that may be insulting and offensive. Name-calling and insulting others are types of verbal aggression and may put the other person on the defensive. This is likely to lead to arguing and could even provoke physical aggression (e.g., fighting).

Along the same lines, avoid all-or-nothing statements (aka black-or-white thinking). When we use words like "always," "never," "everything," and "nothing." we are speaking in extremes. In reality, few things are really black or white; most things are in shades of gray.

We often swear in everyday language without even thinking about it. Part of effective communication is being aware of what you are saying, and this includes being aware of when we use swear words. It is very rare that someone needs to swear, and it is generally thought of as being disrespectful and unhelpful. Furthermore, there are some situations in which it is highly inappropriate to swear—at work in front of your boss, at school in front of the principal or dean, and in court before a judge, for example. In those situations, swearing can result in harsher consequences like being fired, being suspended or expelled, or being taken to juvenile hall.

Making eye contact is also important. It emphasizes what we say, and it is a sign of respect in many cultures. It is much more difficult to be dishonest when you look someone in the eye. Often when we lie or are dishonest, the guilt and shame associated with it prevents us from looking directly at the person. Avoiding eye contact is a possible warning sign.

Finally, our body language should reinforce or support what we say. How we communicate is just as important as what we communicate.

EXERCISE: ACTIVE LISTENING

This exercise should be done with another person. Pick a topic of conversation—for example, some subject in the news or a topic of interest—and have the other person talk about it for two minutes. Then repeat what you heard the speaker say and summarize it. Do not make any judgments or state any opinions. Just reflect back to the other person what he or she said. You might begin with: "I heard you say…." Just reflect back what you heard. Switch roles and repeat this exercise a few times.

EXERCISE: USING "I" STATEMENTS

This exercise should be done with another person. Speaking in the first person—using "I" statements—and owning your feelings is more effective than using "you" statements and blaming. Have a five-minute discussion about something each of you does that irritates the other, and tell each other how you feel using "I" statements, not "you" statements. Use the model below as a guide.

I feel (emotion)_____ when (behavior)_____ takes place.

I feel _____ when _____.

Using "I" statements is especially effective if you want the other person to change a behavior. First, state how you feel and offer a suggestion as to how the person can change the behavior, or state your preference. Do not demand a change in behavior. And remember, you can't change someone else's behavior. Others are more likely to comply with your suggestion if you approach them respectfully. Use the models below.

I feel (emotion)_____ when (behavior)_____ takes place.

I would appreciate it if you _____.

I feel _____ when you _____.

Instead, would you _____?

I feel _____ when you _____.

It would be more helpful if you _____.

Afterward, reflect on the experience. Does it feel more respectful using "I" as opposed to "you?"

EXERCISE: BEING AWARE OF LANGUAGE

This exercise should be done with another person. Pick a topic of conversation—for example, a subject of interest. For five minutes, talk about the subject, with one person using as many all-or-nothing statements as possible. Use words like "always," "never," "everything," and "nothing" as much as possible. Also, engage in name-calling and blaming during the course of the conversation. The other person has to maintain a conversation without making any all-or-nothing statements, name-calling, or blaming. Then discuss this experience for both of you.

Now complete the exercise again in reverse, with the individual who used all-or-nothing thinking, name-calling, and blaming using none of those and the individual who used none using these statements. Again, discuss this experience, and compare and contrast how different the conversations were for each individual. Was it more or less difficult to avoid making all-or-nothing statements, name-calling, and blaming? Did either person, while using no name-calling or blaming, experience feeling defensive or attacked by the other person who did? How does this affect the conversation?

EXERCISE: WATCH THE SWEARING

This exercise can be done alone over the course of two days. To reduce the amount of swearing, we need to be more aware of what we are saying. Once we are aware of what we are saying, we have a choice to use or avoid swear words. We may choose to replace swear words with a less offensive comment—replacing f*** with "fudge," for example. Or we may choose to avoid using inappropriate words altogether, which can alter the intent of the conversation. During the course of one full day, practice being aware of your language. Keep track of the number of times you use swear words throughout the course of a typical day. The next day, practice using no swear words at all. Compare and contrast these two days. Did you find your conversations were more effective, that your communication was better when you watched your language and did not swear? Did you find others approached you differently in conversation?

Evaluate your experiences on both days below.

_____

_____

_____

_____

EXERCISE: BODY LANGUAGE

This exercise should be done with another person. Eye contact and body language are important when talking to one other person or to a whole group, because they either enhance or take away from the topic of conversation. Have a five-minute conversation with someone and note when and how often the individual looks you in the eye, and what his or her body is saying. How does the person sit or stand? Does he or she turn toward you or away from you? What is the person's posture, straight or hunched over? Are the arms in a natural position or crossed in front? Does the person appear nervous or calm? After five minutes, switch and have the other person record your eye contact and body language. Afterward, compare and contrast what you and the other person noticed. Did this add to or take away from the topic? What did you learn?

Write down any thoughts or feelings that came up in this exercise.

_____

_____

_____

_____

_____

_____

_____

Group Discussion Topics for Communication Skills

GROUP DISCUSSION

Have group members discuss their experiences with the active-listening exercises. Do they understand the differences between hearing (mechanics of sound in the ear) and listening (hearing and processing what is said)? Did they find it difficult to listen without interrupting and giving feedback? Did they notice if they felt less defensive or de-personalized the message when using active listening?

GROUP DISCUSSION

Does listening vary in different situations? Does active listening look different in situations in which there is a person of authority (e.g., probation officer, police officer, teacher, parent)? What communication skills are more or less important in these situations?

GROUP DISCUSSION

Discuss the use of body language. What did participants notice about their body language? About their partners' body language? What did they interpret the body language to mean? The group leader can make a list of observations they make about body language and then discuss the subtle or blatant messages they give. Did group members over- or underestimate the importance of body language?

GROUP DISCUSSION

How does using "I" statements instead of "you" statements affect the speaker's message? What about for the person receiving the message? How different is the message when we use "I" vs. "you" statements? Discuss.

Honest Communication Part III—Communication Styles

There are four communication styles: passive, aggressive, passive-aggressive, and assertive. The passive style is driven by fear. The aggressive style is more hostile and threatening. The passive-aggressive style bounces between fear and hostility. In contrast, the assertive style is positive, healthy, and open to considering alternative viewpoints. Most people aspire to have the assertive communication style.

PASSIVE	AGGRESSIVE	PASSIVE-AGRESSIVE	ASSERTIVE
Style: Communication is submissive and compliant Avoids conflict at all costs Communicates in a way that's pleasing to the other person Fear-driven	*Style:* Style is hostile and/or motivated by the desire for power and control May be competitive	*Style:* Communication appears passive at times, but with an unconscious and aggressive motive Denial of personal responsibility in language Fear of conflict	*Style:* Communication is honest and direct Open to others' viewpoints
Belief: Your needs are more important than mine all the time.	*Belief:* My needs are more important than yours. My needs are rights.	*Belief:* Sometimes my needs are more important, but my needs are rights.	*Belief:* My needs and your needs are equally important.
Examples: Talks quietly and without conviction Agrees with everything Avoids eye contact Faces away Hunched, shoulders down	*Examples:* Voice is loud and powerful May be yelling; language may be offensive, insulting, or demeaning Body language and posture may be intimidating	*Examples:* Passive style of communication with episodes of hostile behaviors Appears compliant but with contradictory behaviors May avoid and then be aggressive	*Examples:* Language is direct and specific Makes eye contact Body language shows confidence Positive

Those with the passive communication style put everyone else's needs above their own and often try to please others or avoid disappointing them. Passive individuals tend to communicate in a way that is submissive and compliant, avoiding confrontation or conflict at all costs. They typically speak quietly, may avoid eye contact, may posture away from the person to whom they are speaking, and agree with everything.

Individuals with an aggressive communication style are motivated by their own needs, and do not recognize or acknowledge that others have needs. They are typically motivated by power and control, and may be more confrontational, competitive, and possibly demeaning. Their voices are more likely to be loud and powerful or intimidating. Language may be inappropriate and offensive.

The passive-aggressive communication style fluctuates, in that communication is passive at times and aggressive at others, so it is often unpredictable and conveys a mixed message. Sometimes passive-aggressive individuals communicate in a way that is passive (quiet, pleasing, and submissive); at other times, they may be aggressive, loud, confrontational, and intimidating.

The assertive communication style is most effective in that the message is clear, direct, and honest. Body language is also direct and language is specific. Assertive individuals are open to hearing others' points of view and know that everyone's needs are equally important. Developing an assertive communication style is the goal of learning communication skills. It is the most healthy communication style.

EXERCISE

Answer the following questions:

1. What is your general communication style? Do you identify more with the passive, aggressive, passive-aggressive, or assertive style? Give examples of how you communicate that style.

_____

_____

_____

_____

2. What are your beliefs about your needs and the needs of others?

_____

_____

_____

_____

3. What communication styles are present in your family? Who in your family has a passive style? An aggressive style? A passive-aggressive style? An assertive style? How do you get along with them? How have their styles affected your relationship with them?

_____

_____

_____

_____

4. Where do you think your communication style comes from? What contributed to the development of your communication style?

_____

_____

_____

_____

5. Is your communication style problematic for you? If so, how? Do you want to change how you communicate?

_____

_____

_____

_____

6. How has your communication style affected your substance abuse? And your recovery?

_____

_____

_____

Group Exercise and Discussion Topics for Communication Styles

GROUP EXERCISE

Get into groups of two and have each group role play one of the communication styles. Pairs should be creative and come up with their own scenarios. The other group members can watch and guess which styles the teams are role playing.

GROUP DISCUSSION

Have group members identify their communication styles. Explore what factors have contributed to the development of their individual communication styles; for example, how family members communicate can have an enormous influence on adolescents. Discuss.

GROUP DISCUSSION

How has communication style positively and negatively affected the substance abuse/addiction of group members? As they enter recovery, is there anything they need or want to change about their communication styles?

GROUP DISCUSSION

Sometimes a passive person and an aggressive person will have a relationship, which can result in aggression or domestic violence if certain factors are present. For example, is the aggressive person verbally abusive? Does he or she try to prevent the passive partner from being independent or socializing with friends and family? Is there a dominant vs. submissive interaction in the relationship? Have the group members discuss the dynamics in such a relationship and ask if any of them can relate to this pairing. Some may be in this kind of relationship.

———————————————

Self-Talk

Self-talk refers to how we talk to ourselves, or our internal dialogue. This may be a voice we hear in our own heads or what we say to ourselves out loud. Often, what we tell ourselves is more hurtful and harmful than the things other people say to or about us. How we think about ourselves based on what we've learned, experienced, and been taught molds what we say to ourselves. Self-talk can be negative when, for instance, we say "I am so stupid," which can cause negative feelings like shame, guilt, or embarrassment. How we talk to ourselves can also trigger cravings to use; if we talk to ourselves negatively, we may become depressed or sad, which can trigger the urge to use. Self-talk can also be positive—when we say, for example, "I'm proud of myself" or "I am smart enough," which can, in turn, motivate us and make us feel good. Furthermore, the more we self-talk, the more we believe it, whether the talk is negative or positive. Thus, repetition and reinforcement work.

Explore self-talk through the following exercises. First, identify the feelings that you may have when given negative and positive statements. Then write down the negative and positive self-talk when given a situation.

You may realize that it is much easier to engage in one form of self-talk than another. If it's easier to come up with negative self-talk statements, then you may engage in more negative self-talk than you realize, which can cause depression, sadness, and anger that you may attempt to avoid with drugs. One way to combat the negative self-talk is to change the way you talk to yourself—to become more positive. Again, if you consistently talk to yourself positively, it will become easier and induce positive feelings. If it's easier to come up with positive self-talk statements, then that's great, and it may be a hidden strength. Identify the negative and positive self-talk statements given each of the situations.

EXERCISE

Identify the feelings you may experience when given negative and positive self-talk statements. Then identify negative and positive statements you make and the feelings/emotions associated with them.

NEGATIVE SELF-TALK STATEMENT	FEELINGS/EMOTIONS
I can't do anything right. I don't like anything about myself. I have to be high to have any fun. I can't go a day without using.	

OTHER NEGATIVE STATEMENTS I MAKE	FEELINGS/EMOTIONS

POSITIVE SELF-TALK STATEMENT	FEELINGS/EMOTIONS
I think there are good things about me. I like myself. I want to be clean and sober. I don't have to be high to have fun.	

OTHER POSITIVE STATEMENTS I MAKE	FEELINGS/EMOTIONS

EXERCISE

Identify the negative and positive self-talk statements given each of the situations. Positive self-talk statements can combat the negative statements that may be automatic.

SITUATION	NEGATIVE SELF-TALK	POSITIVE SELF-TALK
Example: You are having difficulty with a subject in school and want to give up.	*Example:* I'm so stupid. I can't do this.	*Example:* If I work hard, I will eventually understand it. I am capable.
You see someone else smoking a blunt, and it causes cravings and urges to use.		
You feel depressed (and want to use).		
You are anxious about an upcoming test and you have to pull an all-nighter to study. You're tempted to take something to keep you up.		
You are really angry and want to smoke some pot to calm you down.		
You have been hanging out with friends who asked you if you wanted to drink. You thought about it, but said "no."		

Group Exercises and Discussion Topics for Self-Talk

GROUP EXERCISE AND DISCUSSION

What we have experienced and learned, both in school and in the home, shapes how we think about ourselves and, in turn, how we talk to ourselves. As a group, make a list of the negative beliefs group members have learned and developed about themselves—for example, negative beliefs about body image or traits. Then make a list of the positive beliefs they have learned and developed about themselves—for example, what they like or appreciate about themselves. Write them down. Are there beliefs that group members have in common? How similar and how different are they? Compare and contrast how these negative and positive beliefs have affected their self-talk and, in turn, their substance use. Does negative self-talk increase the desire to use, or does using increase negative thinking? Discuss.

GROUP EXERCISE

Have group members identify negative thoughts. Then identify the positive counter-statements they can make, writing them on the board as well. Positive self-talk can replace negative self-talk through repetition and reinforcement. Have the group members reflect on this.

GROUP DISCUSSION

Depression is common among substance abusers/addicts, which can increase negative self-talk, negative feelings, and pessimistic mood, and, in turn, perpetuate both problems. Discuss the relationship between depression and substance abuse. Can members relate to this? Does anyone in the group struggle with depression, hopelessness, or anxiety?

GROUP DISCUSSION

Self-talk can be constructive or destructive to recovery. Discuss how negative and positive thinking can be constructive and destructive, respectively. How does this ultimately affect recovery?

7

Managing Emotions

Identifying Emotions

Emotions are controlled by the limbic system, deep within the human brain. Substance use can affect emotions and moods, which, in turn, can affect the type of drugs someone chooses to use and the frequency of use. Furthermore, we often use substances to avoid feeling certain emotions like sadness, anger, or shame. Thus, part of recovery involves identifying, expressing, and coping with emotions.

EXERCISE: IDENTIFYING EMOTIONS
This exercise can be used for individuals or groups. Identify as many emotions as you can, beginning with each letter of the alphabet.

A_____

B_____

C_____

D_____

E_____

F_____

G_____

H_____

I_____

J_____

K_____

L_____

M_____

N_____

O_____

P_____

Q_____

R_____

S_____

T_____

U_____

V_____

W_____

X_____

Y_____

Z_____

EXERCISE: EXPRESSING EMOTIONS

The purpose of this exercise is to become more familiar and comfortable with experiencing and expressing emotions. This exercise can be completed in one of two ways, both of which are explained. In each box below, either draw a face depicting the labeled emotion, or look through magazines for faces depicting the emotions. Cut them out and paste them in the boxes.

HAPPY   CONFIDENT

SAD   ANGRY

SCARED

WORRIED

BORED

CONFUSED

Circle the emotions that are the most comfortable and uncomfortable for you.

The Adolescent Relapse Prevention Planner

Group Exercises and Discussion Topics for Identifying Emotions

GROUP EXERCISE AND DISCUSSION

Have group members work either individually or in small groups. Look through magazines and cut out faces that depict specific emotions. Glue these to paper or poster board, and label the emotions depicted. This can be used as a reference for identifying emotions. Have group members discuss the emotion(s) they find most difficult to access and the easiest. What emotions are tied to their substance abuse? Which of these emotions are triggers for substance use?

GROUP DISCUSSION

Have the group discuss the three emotions that are the most difficult to deal with, and if substance use has been one means of coping with them in the past. What makes these emotions the most difficult? Then, looking at the extensive list of emotions beginning with the letters of the alphabet, are there emotions that are even more difficult to deal with than these three? For example, someone may list anger as the most difficult emotion. How do people cope with these additional emotions?

GROUP DISCUSSION

Discuss the idea that substance abusers and addicts use either *to feel* something (e.g., the high, have fun) or *to avoid feeling* something (e.g., sadness, anger). Do group members agree or disagree with this, and what is it that fuels use for each member—using to feel or to avoid feeling?

GROUP EXERCISE

Have group members make a collage of feelings (using magazines) that they experience on an everyday basis. They may struggle with numerous negative emotions, a mixture of positive and negative emotions, or a few emotions that are more likely to trigger or fuel substance abuse. This is a great way of expressing what is inside without having to talk about the emotions at length. This may be particularly helpful with adolescents who have difficulty opening up. Afterward, they may share their collages with the group or in individual therapy.

Coping with Difficult Emotions—Shame

For some people, it is easy to access and express emotions; for others, it may be very difficult. There are many reasons for this. Some people are more logic-oriented; others may be numb from past experiences and traumas and avoid or suppress emotional expression. Some may hold on to the false notion that showing emotions is a weakness. In contrast, some people are overly emotional and have difficulty managing their emotions. Furthermore, substance abusers and addicts often use either *to feel* (e.g., excitement or happiness with the high) or *to avoid feeling* (e.g., sadness, vulnerability, shame). Part of recovery is learning to identify, express, and cope with difficult emotions.

Shame is an uncomfortable emotion for most people—in part, because it is often tied to other emotions like anger and can leave us feeling vulnerable. Sometimes individuals use substances to avoid feeling shame about something in their past over which they may or may not have had any control. Sometimes they are trying to avoid a present circumstance or condition, and/or an aspect of themselves they are uncomfortable with—negative body image, low self-esteem, or low self-worth. Shame can fuel substance abuse, which, in turn, can become a source of shame that keeps the user trapped.

EXERCISE

Answer the following questions:

1. Have you ever struggled with feeling shame? If so, when? What was that like? What caused or contributed to feeling ashamed?

   _____

   _____

   _____

2. Sometimes traumatic events in childhood (e.g., physical, sexual, or emotional abuse; domestic violence; bullying; accidents) can be a source of shame, whether we are aware of it or not. Have you experienced any such events that you think may have directly caused or contributed to your feelings of shame?

   _____

   _____

   _____

3. Low self-esteem, low self-worth, or self-hatred can make us feel ashamed as well. Sometimes it can be caused by these traumatic events, sometimes by other things like peer pressure or differences with classmates. Do you struggle with low self-esteem, low self-worth, or self-hatred? If so, how has this affected your life?

_____

_____

_____

4. How have you coped with feelings of shame? Did you or have you ever used substances to avoid feeling shame?

_____

_____

_____

5. Substance abuse can cause feelings of shame or magnify them in those who already experience shame prior to use. Have you felt ashamed about your substance use?

_____

_____

_____

6. What are some other ways of coping with feelings of shame?

_____

_____

_____

Group Exercise and Discussion Topics for Coping with Shame

GROUP EXERCISE AND DISCUSSION

Pass out one index card per person if you have a large group; two index cards per person if you have a small group. Have group members write one thing of which they are ashamed (I am ashamed of _____). Tell group members not to write their names on the cards. Collect all the cards, put them in a bowl, and mix them up. Pick one card at a time, and have the group discuss what was written on the card. Can group members relate? If so, how? What may have contributed to this feeling of shame? Could the shame be trauma-based? Discuss several cards depending upon the time.

GROUP DISCUSSION

Have the group discuss their experiences of shame around admitting they have a problem with substance abuse and/or addiction. What was it like for the first time to admit they had a problem with substances? What makes substance abuse/addiction so shameful? How can they overcome this shame and focus on recovery? Is recovery or being clean and sober something to be proud of? Why or why not?

GROUP DISCUSSION

Adolescents—girls especially—may experience a lot of shame around their bodies and appearance, in part, due to the media's focus on beauty and "the perfect body." This may, in turn, fuel substance use, addiction, eating disorders, body-image problems, or even self-harm (e.g., cutting). Discuss how shame about ourselves may fuel substance use. Do any of the group members struggle with this, and how? Are drugs a means of avoiding feelings? A form of weight loss? A means to become more social and popular? What can group members do to work through this shame?

Coping with Difficult Emotions—Guilt

Guilt can be a complicated emotion, similar to shame. Guilt may best be described as feeling bad about or regretting something that we shouldn't have done or wish we had done differently. Guilt often occurs in combination with remorse when we realize the negative effects of our actions. However, guilt can also come about when we wish we had acted differently, whether or not what we did was wrong. Sometimes we feel guilty for doing what's right! Guilt can be self-induced or imposed on us by someone else (guilt-tripping) like a parent or friend. For example, we can make ourselves feel guilty for lying to our parents. Similar to shame, guilt can fuel substance use, which, in turn, can become a source of guilt and a trigger to use even more.

EXERCISE
Answer the following questions:

1. Have you struggled with guilt in your life? Do you currently struggle with guilt about something you have said or done? If so, what?

   _____

   _____

   _____

2. Do you feel guilty about your substance abuse or about things you did while you were using? For example, did you lie about the drug use or steal money for drugs? How has this guilt affected you?

   _____

   _____

   _____

3. Is the guilt valid or are you really just being hard on yourself?

   _____

   _____

   _____

4. How can you reduce the guilt?

   _____

   _____

   _____

5. What messages do you give yourself that increase your feelings of guilt? For example, do you tell yourself "I'm not good enough," "I'm not smart enough," or "I'm a loser"? Write down the messages you give yourself that probably bring about or increase feelings of guilt.

_____

_____

_____

_____

_____

_____

6. Do these messages help you or harm you?

_____

_____

_____

Group Discussion Topics for Coping with Guilt

GROUP EXERCISE AND DISCUSSION

As a group, explore the questions posed in the following Parts 1–3.

Part 1:
When we abuse substances, we sometimes do things that we would not otherwise do (e.g., steal, lie, cheat, hurt others). We may not feel guilty at the time, but when we are in recovery, we may remember or become aware of what we did and how we hurt others, producing guilt. Discuss how individuals in the group experience guilt, how guilt has affected them, and what caused the guilt.

Part 2:
Discuss how this guilt affected the group members' substance use. Were the behaviors that produced guilt directly or indirectly related to their substance abuse? Did the guilt lead to more substance use or less? People sometimes use drugs to hide the guilt, fueling the drug use, and, in turn, increasing guilt. Can group members relate?

Part 3:

Recovery often requires that we "right the wrongs" we have done (compensate). It may be as simple as apologizing to someone we hurt, paying for damage we caused, or replacing something we took, for example. Discuss the importance and role of compensation in recovery. How does this affect the guilt?

GROUP DISCUSSION

There is a saying: "Guilt kills." Discuss what this means and how it affects substance abuse and recovery.

GROUP DISCUSSION

What is the difference between guilt and shame, and how are they related?

GROUP EXERCISE: APOLOGY LETTER

Have group members identify something they feel guilty about (e.g., robbing someone, hurting a family member, lying to parents, damaging someone's property). Identify who was affected by their action (or inaction), and how they were affected. Then have them write apology letters to the person(s) who were affected, hurt, damaged, etc. Include how they may "make up for" or "make right" their behaviors. Afterward, the letters should be given to the actual person(s) in order to reduce guilt and shame associated with past actions. Discuss these experiences during the next group.

Coping with Difficult Emotions—Depression

Depression may affect emotions and moods. Depression is a little different for everyone, but it is often characterized by sadness, pessimism, negativity, hopelessness, anger, and/or a lack of pleasure. Depression may affect someone physically with symptoms that include fatigue or exhaustion, body aches and pains, changes in sleeping patterns, and changes in appetite and/or eating. Depression may become a disorder if it lasts for an extended period of time and interferes with daily functioning. Depression can affect substance use and vice versa.

EXERCISE

Answer the following questions:

1. Have you ever struggled with feeling depressed? Did/do you feel sad, angry, hopeless, and/or pessimistic?

    _____

    _____

    _____

2. Did/do you experience any of the physical symptoms of depression? If so, what?

    _____

    _____

    _____

3. Did/do you have difficulty experiencing pleasure or fun? Can you give an example? Were/are you able to look forward to anything?

    _____

    _____

    _____

4. If you struggled with depression, when was it and how long did it last? Do you currently struggle with depression? Have you experienced depression more than once? Have you ever been diagnosed with depression or bipolar depression?

    _____

    _____

    _____

5. Do you know what caused the depressed feelings? Was it multiple little things or one major incident like the death of a loved one? Explain.

_____

_____

_____

6. How did/do you cope with feeling depressed (good and bad)? Did/do you ever use substances to avoid feeling depressed?

_____

_____

_____

7. Has depression contributed to your substance abuse? Has depression led to an increase or decrease in substance use? Has substance use contributed to your depressed feelings?

_____

_____

_____

8. Do you have family members with depression? If so, who?

_____

_____

Group Exercise and Discussion Topics for Coping with Depression

GROUP DISCUSSION

Depression may be experienced intensely for a limited amount of time, leading to a diagnosis of major depression, or at a lower, less intense level but for a longer period of time, as with dysthymia. Depression will sometimes contribute to or fuel substance abuse. Or depression may alternate with periods of mania or hypomania. Regardless, depression and drug use may go hand in hand. Discuss the role of depression in the lives of group members. Do some currently struggle with depression, or have they in the past? How is the depression related to their substance abuse? Do depressed feelings increase or decrease substance use? Does substance use increase feelings of depression? How can someone escape this cycle of substance use and depression?

GROUP DISCUSSION

Substance abuse/addiction may produce a deficit in the brain's chemicals, leading to the possibility of long-term depression. (Certain drugs like ecstasy or meth cause an overabundance followed by a depletion of the neurotransmitters serotonin and dopamine, which are responsible for mood.) Some individuals may, in turn, be prescribed anti-depressants for depression. What are the pros and cons of taking medications in recovery? Some may see it as a quick fix, but is it? Is medication for depression ever justified in adolescents? Why or why not?

GROUP EXERCISE AND DISCUSSION

Guilt, shame, and depression are sometimes experienced separately and sometimes together. On a board or large piece of butcher paper, make a list with three columns, listing what causes or contributes to feelings of guilt, shame, and depression (e.g., trauma, violence, low self-esteem, negative body image). Circle the factors that cause all three. Then make a fourth column for ways of coping with these feelings. Are these factors also triggers for substance use? Discuss this possible connection. Make a separate list of how to cope with these factors/triggers.

Coping with Difficult Emotions—Fear

Fear is one of those emotions we tend to ignore when we are using, but it "rears its ugly head" during the recovery process. Often, we do not acknowledge fear or we minimize fear and its effects—possibly because it is uncomfortable, appears embarrassing, or makes us feel vulnerable and threatened. Fear may take on different forms, and may trigger substance use as we try to avoid or escape our fears through drinking, drug-using, or acting out in general. We may have legitimate fears for our safety and survival. Maybe we have an abusive parent, relative, or boyfriend/girlfriend. Or we may live in a violent poverty-stricken neighborhood or have serious, life-threatening health problems. We may develop fears of flashbacks or unwanted memories of traumatic events in our lives. We can have fears of individuals (e.g., violent partners) or groups of people (e.g., terrorist organizations). We may have fears of conditions or things (e.g., phobias) or fears of the unknown (what would happen if we stopped using) or of the future. Some fears may become apparent in recovery, like the fear of failure (fearing treatment failure) or the fear of success (surviving treatment and living a clean and sober lifestyle). Fears may be real or imagined, or we may overreact and exacerbate fears of dying, having a heart attack, or having a stroke, for example, which can induce panic attacks. The panic feels real, but fuels further panic. Some fears may be minimized because they feel overwhelming, frightening, or impossible to overcome, which gives us an excuse to use.

Exercise

Answer the following questions about fear by marking the statements that are true for you:

Fears about physical safety and security:

_____ I fear someone in my life who has hit and/or physically harmed me.

_____ I fear someone/something may physically hurt me.

_____ I fear someone who has threatened me physically.

_____ I fear being bullied.

_____ I fear someone who bullies me.

_____ I fear violence.

_____ I fear someone/something may sexually harm (e.g., rape, molest, sexually abuse) me.

_____ I fear being sexually abused (e.g., raped, molested).

_____ I am scared for my life.

_____ I fear for my family's safety.

_____ I fear I and/or my family will be homeless.

_____ I fear poverty.

_____ I fear death and/or dying.

_____ I fear _____.

Fears about emotional safety, security, and stability:

_____ I fear someone who has hurt me emotionally by saying things that are mean, hurtful, or belittling to me.

_____ I fear someone who has threatened me emotionally.

_____ I fear someone close to me turning his or her back on me.

_____ I fear being rejected/rejection.

_____ I fear being alone.

_____ I fear getting close to someone.

_____ I fear being attached to someone.

_____ I fear commitment.

_____ I fear failure (of any kind).

_____ I fear success/achieving my goals.

_____ I fear not living up to my or my parents' expectations.

_____ I fear _____.

Fears about conditions/things:

_____ I fear heights.

_____ I fear small or enclosed spaces.

_____ I fear crowds or lots of people.

_____ I fear social situations.

_____ I fear leaving my house.

_____ I fear being trapped or unable to leave a situation.

_____ I fear water (e.g., the ocean, swimming pools, lakes, etc).

_____ I fear weight gain.

_____ I fear being ugly.

_____ I fear certain foods.

_____ I fear bugs and/or spiders.

_____ I fear trains, planes, cars, or other forms of transportation.

_____ I fear flying, driving, sailing, or other forms of transportation.

_____ I fear needles and/or blood.

_____ I fear darkness/night.

_____ I fear the future.

_____ I fear males, females, or specific groups of people.

_____ I fear _____.

Fears about disease, illness, or death that are real or imagined:

_____ I fear dying.

_____ I fear pain.

_____ I fear germs.

_____ I fear hospitals and/or doctors' offices.

_____ I am scared of having a heart attack or stroke.

_____ I am afraid of having a panic attack or anxiety attack.

_____ I am scared of being or getting sick.

_____ I am scared of developing a serious physical illness (e.g., cancer, leukemia, liver disease, diabetes, etc.).

_____ I am afraid of contracting an STD, AIDS, or HIV.

_____ I am afraid of developing a serious mental illness (e.g., schizophrenia, bipolar disorder, depression, Alzheimer's disease, etc.).

_____ I am afraid of _____.

Fears about addiction, relapse, or recovery:

_____ I fear I may have a substance abuse problem and/or be an addict.

_____ I am afraid of using "hard drugs."

_____ I fear relapse.

_____ I am afraid of going through withdrawal.

_____ I am afraid of going into a treatment facility/seeking treatment.

_____ I fear I may never be able to drink or use again.

_____ I fear _____.

Answer the following questions about the fears you have identified:

1. What fears did you identify, and in what category did the majority of your fears fall?

   _____
   _____
   _____

2. Are your fears real or imagined or both? Explain.

   _____
   _____
   _____

3. What fears are real or based on real-life experiences?

   _____
   _____
   _____

4. What may have caused or contributed to these fears (e.g., events, people, places, things, etc.)?

   _____
   _____
   _____

5. What fears are imagined, based on "worst-case scenarios," or negative thinking?

   _____
   _____
   _____

6. What may have caused or contributed to these fears?

_____

_____

_____

7. Are you willing to work on or have you begun working on changing these fears? How?

_____

_____

_____

Group Exercise and Discussion Topics for Coping with Fear

GROUP EXERCISE

This exercise is similar to the first exercise about shame. Pass out index cards, and have group members write their biggest fears on them (My biggest fear is _____). Again, do not have them write their names. Gather the cards and mix them up; draw the cards one by one and discuss each fear. Write the fears on a board. Discuss each fear and strategize what may have caused or contributed to its development. Are any of the fears trauma-based (or based on traumatic incidents from the past)? Then strategize what can be done or changed to overcome this fear or make it more manageable. Write the strategies on the board.

GROUP DISCUSSION

Discuss in depth each category of fears, and which fears were identified by multiple group members. How have group members learned to cope (positively or negatively) with these fears? Discuss:

- Fear for physical safety and security
- Fear for emotional safety and security
- Fear of conditions or things
- Fear of disease, illness, or death
- Fear of addiction, relapse, or recovery

GROUP DISCUSSION

Have group members discuss the difference between real and imagined fears. What makes fears real or imagined, and what causes these fears? Did some identify themselves as having imagined fears? How do we convince ourselves that imagined fears are real fears? (Hint: Think about panic attacks.)

GROUP DISCUSSION

Discuss how fears drive, cause, or contribute to substance use/addiction. Do some use, for example, to avoid feeling or dealing with their fears? Have any fears developed as a result of their substance use? How can fears prevent individuals from living clean and sober?

Managing Anger

Anger is a difficult emotion for some people—maybe because it is associated with negative qualities (like violence), because it feels overwhelming or uncontrollable, or because it may be difficult to access and feels too threatening. However, anger is really a secondary emotion. For a lot of people, anger is more easily accessible than the sadness, hurt, shame, or guilt that lies beneath it. Anger, in and of itself, is not a bad thing; it's how we behave when angry that often leads to problems. For people who have difficulty controlling their reactions to anger, they may benefit from learning anger-management skills. Teenagers often fall into this category. Anger management includes building an awareness of your anger, learning to express anger in non-aggressive and non-abusive ways, and learning to cope with the feelings underneath. To develop an awareness of anger involves identifying triggers and recognizing the physical, cognitive, and emotional symptoms of anger.

EXERCISE: DO I HAVE AN ANGER PROBLEM?
Answer the following questions. Circle "T" if the statement is True for you and circle "F" if the statement is False or does not pertain to you.

T F   I get angry easily and quickly.

T F   It's hard for me to calm down when I get angry.

T F   I feel angry every day about something.

T F   People tell me I have an anger problem.

T F   My anger sometimes feels uncontrollable and/or overwhelming.

T F   When I get angry, I feel powerful or superior.

T F   I store up my anger until I explode.

T F   I feel enraged at times.

T F   When I get angry with others, I sometimes want revenge.

T F   When I get angry, I sometimes behave badly.

In the past, at least once, when I was angry, I did the following:

T F   I hit something (e.g., punching bag, pillow, wall, door).

T F   I hurt myself hitting someone or something.

T F   I threw something.

T F   I kicked something or someone.

T F   I yelled and/or screamed.

T F   I was verbally hurtful to someone (insulted, cursed).

T F   I scared myself or someone.

T F   I purposely hurt myself physically—for example, cut or burned myself.

If you answered "T" (True) to any of these statements, you may struggle with anger problems and/or have anger-management problems. The more "T"s you mark, the more likely it is that you have problems with anger.

Now reflect on your answers and answer these questions:

1. How many times did you answer True, and does this surprise you?

   _____

   _____

2. Have you become physically aggressive when angry (e.g., hit or kicked something or someone, thrown something, fought)? What did you do? How did you feel afterward?

   _____

   _____

3. Have you tried to manage or control your anger in the past? How?

   _____

   _____

EXERCISE: HOW DO YOU EXPERIENCE ANGER?

Put a check in each box that applies to you.

When I get angry, I experience (or have experienced) the following physical symptoms:

☐ tension   ☐ shakiness or tremor   ☐ muscle spasms   ☐ headache

☐ tightness in the neck or shoulders   ☐ clenched fists

☐ changes in temperature (hot or cold)   ☐ problems breathing

☐ stomach cramps or "butterflies"   ☐ nausea   ☐ tightened jaw

☐ increased heart rate or heart palpitations   ☐ racing thoughts

☐ blackouts or loss of consciousness   ☐ other _____

When I get angry (or immediately after), I have experienced the following emotional symptoms:

☐ I cry.   ☐ I panic.   ☐ I want to cry but can't seem to.

☐ I feel sadness.   ☐ I feel ashamed or embarrassed.

☐ I feel guilty.   ☐ I feel vulnerable.   ☐ I don't remember what I did.

☐ I feel bad.   ☐ I feel good.   ☐ I feel _____.

What do these physical and emotional symptoms tell you about how you experience your anger?

_____

_____

_____

Have you ever used drugs to control these symptoms?

_____

_____

_____

EXERCISE: WHAT TRIGGERS YOUR ANGER?

Circle "T" for True or "F" for False, as these statements pertain to you and your anger.

T F   I get angry when I feel disrespected or someone is disrespectful.

T F   I get angry when I am lied to or insulted, and/or when someone makes
            rude or insulting comments.

T F   I get angry when I feel criticized or judged, and/or when someone is critical or
            judgemental.

T F   I get angry when I feel ignored, and/or when someone avoids or ignores something
            important.

T F   I get angry when I feel cheated, and/or when someone cheats.

T F   I get angry when I feel helpless or powerless.

T F   I get angry when I feel threatened (physically or emotionally), and/or when some-
            one I care about feels threatened.

T F   I get angry when someone makes inappropriate and/or prejudicial remarks about
            race, ethnicity, culture, sex, or sexual preferences.

T F   I get angry when someone or something seems unfair.

T F   I get angry when my belongings are stolen, and/or when someone takes something
            that doesn't belong to them.

T F   I get angry when I am physically or emotionally hurt, and/or when someone I care
            about is hurt.

T F   I get angry when I lose (a game, contest).

T F   I get angry when someone is lazy or procrastinates.

T F   I get angry when I think someone acts stupidly.

T F   I get angry when I have to wait.

These are triggers related to people, some of which are internal sources of anger—feelings, thoughts, sensations, and perceptions that are within us—while others are more external or dependent on others. Internal sources like what we feel may be easier to control, whereas external sources may be less controllable.

EXERCISE: WHAT SITUATIONS TRIGGER ANGER? TO WHAT HAVE WE BEEN EXPOSED?
Circle "T" for True and "F" for False as these statements pertain to you and your anger.

T F   Seeing or hearing prejudice of any kind makes me angry.

T F   I have experienced prejudice at least once in my life.

T F   Seeing or hearing about child abuse (physical, sexual, emotional) makes me angry.

T F   I have experienced physical, sexual, or emotional abuse at least once in my life.

T F   Seeing or hearing about domestic violence/spousal abuse (physical, sexual, emotional abuse by a spouse, partner, boyfriend, girlfriend) makes me angry.

T F   I or someone I care about has experienced domestic violence/spousal abuse at least once.

T F   Seeing or hearing about animal abuse makes me angry.

T F   I have witnessed physical abuse of an animal.

T F   Seeing or hearing about gang-related violence of any kind makes me angry.

T F   I am gang-affiliated and/or someone I care about is gang-affiliated.

T F   Seeing or hearing about violence on the streets—robbery, burglary, assault, rape, or murder—makes me angry.

T F   I have experienced violence on the streets at least once.

T F   I have been the victim of crime at least once in my life.

T F   Homelessness makes me angry.

T   F   I have been homeless for a period of time.

T   F   I have been "on the run" for a period of time.

T   F   Seeing or hearing about war makes me angry.

T   F   I have experienced war first-hand in some way.

T   F   Seeing or hearing about terrorism makes me angry.

T   F   I have experienced terrorism or its effects in my life.

These triggers are situations that are, for the most part, not under our control, and are therefore external to us. However, our response to these situations now can be influenced by our experiences of these situations in the past. For example, we may be more reactive or defensive to seeing or hearing about child abuse if we have experienced child abuse personally. Problem-solving, conflict negotiation, and mediation are strategies we can use to manage our anger better emotionally and physically, and to decrease the likelihood of substance use as well.

EXERCISE: IDENTIFYING COPING SKILLS TO MANAGE ANGER

Problem-solving:

I am willing to try the following problem-solving strategies to manage my anger better:

_____ Talk to a supportive person.

_____ Be honest about my feelings.

_____ Allow myself to work through the feelings underneath my anger.

_____ Avoid personalizing the issue.

_____ Write, journal, or draw.

_____ Distract myself and talk about it later.

_____ Take a "time-out" by giving myself space and time to think things through (take a walk, sit outside, etc.).

_____ Try a relaxation exercise.

_____ Try deep breathing.

_____ Work out my physical tension through exercise like playing ball, running, lifting weights, etc.

_____ Walk away or leave the situation.

Conflict negotiation:

I am willing to try the following conflict-negotiation and/or mediation strategies to manage my anger better:

_____ Talk about what is making me angry with someone with whom I am in conflict.

_____ Negotiate a resolution in which each person in conflict "gives up a little" so that both sides get at least some of what they want.

_____ Let go of the desire to have the last word.

Mediation:

_____ Have a neutral person listen to both sides and help to negotiate a solution.

_____ Agree to disagree.

_____ See a therapist.

Group Exercises and Discussion Topics for Anger Management

GROUP EXERCISE: DEEP BREATHING

Have the group sit or lie down in a comfortable position with their eyes open or closed. Lead them through the following steps:

Breathe in through your mouth for four seconds. As you inhale, fill your lungs and torso with air. You can put your hands on your stomach, and feel it expand with each inhalation. Do not breathe in through your nose. Hold the breath for another four seconds. Then exhale for eight seconds, pushing all the air out of your diaphragm through your mouth. Repeat this exercise several times, remembering to count four seconds in-breath, four seconds hold, and eight seconds out-breath. Keep repeating this exercise—counting 'four, four, eight'—until you feel calmer and less stressed.

GROUP DISCUSSION

Reacting to anger with physical aggression is often a learned behavior. Maybe you witnessed an adult (i.e., parent) hitting another adult, or a parent hitting a child (maybe you). These experiences can directly or indirectly teach you to be aggressive. How do group members feel about this? What do they think about the concept of violence as a learned behavior? How many of them can relate to this and/or see their own aggressive acts as learned behaviors? How can aggression be "unlearned?" Discuss.

GROUP DISCUSSION

Discuss the connection between anger and substance abuse. Sometimes adolescents use alcohol or drugs to cover up their anger and, even more so, to avoid the underlying feelings. Others use substances to calm themselves down. Does this help or hurt in the long run? How?

GROUP EXERCISE: DEBATE

Entertainment in the form of television, movies, video games, and music seem to depict a lot of violence—which, it may be argued, increases violent behaviors. This may be supported by higher rates in violent crime. Have the group members debate this topic: Do children who are exposed to violence in TV shows, movies, video games, and music grow up to be more violent?

8

Maintaining a Clean and Sober Lifestyle

Stress Management

Stress is a difficult concept to define—in part, because everyone experiences stress differently. Most agree, however, that stress can be harmful and usually results from physical, psychological, and emotional states that appear to be threatening. When individuals perceive a threat to their survival or well-being, the body and brain respond by going into a fight-or-flight response (i.e., the individuals either fight or flee). Adrenalin and cortisol are released and the sympathetic nervous system is excited, causing a variety of reactions in the body, like an increase in heart rate and blood pressure and a surge of energy. Short-term or acute stress can be beneficial at times when we need a burst of energy to complete a task—like studying for a test or running a marathon—and when we need to escape from a dangerous situation. However, long-term, chronic stress is detrimental, as the body and mind are tricked into thinking we are always in fight-or-flight mode. This taxes the body's immune system, making us more susceptible to heart attacks, strokes, and fatigue, and to minor illnesses (flu, colds) and major diseases (cardiovascular disease, rheumatoid arthritis, depression, anxiety disorders) (Rosch, 1989; Rosch, 1983; Selye, 1946).

EXERCISE

Complete the exercise below by marking the physical, psychological, or emotional effects of stress that you have experienced. This will give you a better understanding of the effects of stress on your life that may have been triggers to use substances.

Short-term effects:

___ Increased heart rate   ___ Blood-clotting problems

___ Increased blood pressure   ___ Hormonal changes

___ Headache

___ Migraine

___ Neck pain

___ Muscle spasms

___ Anxiety, nervousness

___ Difficulty sleeping

___ Bad dreams

___ Fatigue or tiredness

___ Adrenalin rush

___ Burst of energy

___ Fidgeting

___ Inability to sit still

___ Difficulty breathing

___ Panic attacks

___ Hyperventilating

___ Hypervigilance

___ Frequent illnesses (colds, flu)

___ Weight loss or weight gain

___ Nausea, vomiting, diarrhea

___ Menstrual problems

___ Hair loss

___ Back pain

___ Tremors

___ Restlessness

___ Excessive worrying

___ Mood swings

___ Dizziness or lightheadedness

___ Obsessive thinking

___ Forgetfulness

___ Disorganized thinking

___ Confusion or indecisiveness

___ Difficulty concentrating

___ Impaired judgment

___ Depression

___ Feeling overwhelmed

___ Appetite changes

___ Irritability or moodiness

___ Frustration

___ Constipation

___ Rash

___ Itching

___ Changes in temperature

___ Flushing

___ Dilated pupils

___ Decreased immunity to illness

___ Sexual problems (impotence, premature ejaculation)

___ Highly reactive behavior or defensiveness

___ Temperamental swings

___ Racing thoughts

___ Increased startle response

___ Fear

___ Anger

___ Hostility or aggression

___ Heart palpitations

___ Stomach pains, heartburn, indigestion, or acid reflux

___ Compulsive behaviors (drinking, drugs, eating, gambling, shopping, having sex, cutting, self-harming)

Long-term effects:

___ High blood pressure

___ Heart attack

___ Irregular heart beat

___ High cholesterol

___ Stroke

___ Ulcers

___ Gastrointestinal problems

___ Depression

___ Anxiety disorders

___ OCD

___ Addiction

___ Panic disorder

___ Eating disorders

___ Obesity

___ Hormonal problems   ___ Autoimmune disease

___ Cancer   ___ PTSD

EXERCISE

Identify ten everyday situations in your life that cause short-term stress and consider how you can manage the short-term, temporary stress.

SITUATIONS	COPING STRATEGIES
Example: Math test	Study for limited time with breaks
Example: Missing the bus after school	Walk home
_____	_____
_____	_____
_____	_____
_____	_____
_____	_____
_____	_____
_____	_____
_____	_____
_____	_____
_____	_____
_____	_____
_____	_____
_____	_____
_____	_____
_____	_____
_____	_____

EXERCISE

List five situations or problems that can cause long-term, chronic stress in your life, followed by five coping strategies you have used, positive and negative.

SITUATIONS/PROBLEMS	COPING STRATEGIES
Example: Parents' divorce	Talking to a counselor or friend
_____	_____
_____	_____
_____	_____
_____	_____
_____	_____

EXERCISE

Look at the ways you have coped with short-term or long-term stress. Some coping strategies for chronic stress may be positive (e.g., doing yoga, exercising, asking for help), and some may be negative (e.g., doing drugs, fighting). Identify which of these coping skills are positive. These are the skills you probably want to continue using as a clean and sober person.

POSITIVE COPING STRATEGIES	NEGATIVE COPING STRATEGIES
_____	_____
_____	_____
_____	_____
_____	_____
_____	_____

EXERCISE

Answer the following questions based on your responses:

1. How do negative strategies affect your stress level? Do they increase or decrease your stress level?

   _____

   _____

   _____

2. How do positive strategies affect your stress level? Do they increase or decrease your stress level?

   _____

   _____

   _____

3. What does this tell you about positive vs. negative coping strategies?

_____

_____

_____

Group Exercise and Discussion Topics for Stress Management

GROUP EXERCISE: VISUALIZATION

This exercise is appropriate for both individuals and groups. When feeling stressed, this visualization may help to reduce the stress and increase calmness.

Sit or lie down in a comfortable position. Clear your mind of all your worries, concerns, thoughts, and fears. Imagine a leaf falling from a tree in the autumn. The leaf is propelled back and forth with a gentle breeze. It floats left to right and right to left, gently and slowly. The leaf is as light as a feather and just keeps floating down to the ground. Continue imagining this leaf floating to the ground until you are calm and relaxed. After several minutes, it finally comes to rest on the ground among the other fallen leaves. (Sit silently for a few minutes visualizing the leaf).

After the visualization, have the group reflect on their experiences of it.

GROUP DISCUSSION

Situations that provoke stress can often be some of the same situations that trigger substance abusers to use alcohol and drugs. Thus, there may be an overlap in identifying drug triggers and stress triggers. Discuss how stress can be a trigger for using substances. What conclusions can the group make in discussing the connection between drugs and stress and their triggers?

GROUP DISCUSSION

Discuss the importance of stress prevention. How can individuals prevent these little, everyday stressful situations? How can individuals prevent chronic long-term stress? Does anyone in the group already practice stress-prevention techniques? How does this relate to substance abuse?

GROUP DISCUSSION

What situations or problems did group members identify as causing stress? How many of these situations are under their own control? How many of these situations are caused by someone else? In other words, who has the locus of control in these situations? Why does locus of control matter? Does it affect how we choose to cope with these situations?

_____

Self-Care

Taking care of yourself physically, psychologically, and emotionally is very important in maintaining a clean and sober lifestyle. Behaviors we engage in to take care of ourselves are positive, healthy, and adaptive. You may have identified some of these coping strategies already in the previous exercises on stress. When we are using, however—especially during binges that last for days or even weeks—we often neglect basic self-care.

We may be too busy using or coming down to take care of basic hygiene—showering, brushing our teeth, or shaving, for example. We may not eat healthy foods, or even eat at all (which is common on meth binges), and we probably are not getting the vitamins, minerals, or nutrients our bodies need. We may not properly hydrate, exercise, or sleep. Part of the recovery process, is "catching up" and getting back to a healthier, more balanced lifestyle. When we don't take care of ourselves, these are warning signs of relapse.

EXERCISE

Answer the questions below, and check all that apply:

When I was using, there were periods of time when I:

___ Didn't shower or bathe   ___ Didn't eat or drink

___ Didn't wash my face   ___ Didn't eat healthy foods

___ Didn't wash my hair   ___ Had the "munchies"

___ Didn't brush or comb my hair ___ Drank too much caffeine

___ Didn't brush my teeth   ___ Ate too much sugar

___ Didn't shave   ___ Didn't take vitamins

___ Didn't change my clothes   ___ Didn't take prescribed meds

___ Didn't wash my clothes   ___ Didn't take birth control

___ Didn't exercise   ___ Had unprotected sex

___ Didn't walk   ___ Skipped medical appointments

___ Didn't sleep   ___ Smoked cigarettes

___ Stayed up for long periods of time

How did these behaviors, or in some cases, lack of self-care behaviors, affect your overall health?

_____

_____

_____

_____

EXERCISE

Recovery involves self-care on a regular basis. Check all self-care behaviors that apply to you. Then write a **D** next to those activities that you engage in daily, a **W** next to those you engage in weekly, and an **I** next to those you do infrequently or less often.

Recovery means I need to do the following:

_____ Shower/bathe   _____ Eat healthy foods

_____ Wash my hair   _____ Eat breakfast

_____ Brush/comb my hair   _____ Eat lunch

_____ Brush my teeth and floss   _____ Eat dinner

_____ Shave   _____ Take vitamins

_____ Wash my clothes   _____ Take prescribed medications

_____ Exercise   _____ Sleep eight hours

_____ Meditate   _____ Attend medical/dental
                                            appointments, including therapy

Part of self-care also involves learning and practicing coping skills to maintain a more balanced lifestyle that includes activities that make us feel good. Everyone uses different self-care strategies—some more social-oriented or extroverted, and others more individualized or introverted.

Extroverts relax, rejuvenate, and re-energize through interactions with other people or social activities like going out with friends, dancing, or playing group sports. In contrast, introverts relax, rejuvenate, and re-energize through more solitary activities like reading, writing, or meditating. These extrovert/introvert traits often fall along a continuum—at one end are extroverts, and at the other end are introverts. Some people find themselves at the extremes, whereas others find they do both and rate themselves as being more in the middle. Being extroverted or introverted tells us a lot about how we can take care of ourselves. Distraction is a basic self-care strategy and may be related to tendencies toward extroversion and introversion.

EXERCISE

Answer the following questions about the extroversion/introversion continuum:

1. Where do you rate yourself on the extrovert/introvert continuum? Why?

Extrovert <————————————> Introvert

_____

_____

_____

2. In what types of extrovert activities do you engage?

_____

_____

_____

_____

3. In what types of introvert activities do you engage?

_____

_____

_____

_____

4. Did you engage in more extroverted drug use (e.g., using at parties, using with people) or more introverted drug use (e.g., using alone)? What does this tell you about your drug use and your recovery?

_____

_____

_____

_____

EXERCISE

Below is a comprehensive list of adaptive coping strategies—some extroverted, some introverted, some general, some very specific. Identify which coping skills you use by putting a check on the line. Also, indicate how often you engage in these coping skills by writing a **D** if daily, **W** if weekly, and **I** if infrequently to the right.

___Aerobics	___Afterschool activities
___Applying to colleges	___Attending AA or NA
___Babysitting	___Baseball
___Basketball	___Biking
___Blogging	___Boxing
___Calling a friend	___Camping
___Ceramics	___Cleaning
___Cooking/baking	___Creative writing
___Dancing	___Designing
___Doing arts and crafts	___Doing chores
___Doing laundry	___Drawing
___Driving	___Dusting

___Exercising

___Gardening

___Going out with friends

___Going to the beach

___Going to therapy

___Golf

___Hiking

___Jogging

___Karaoke

___Listening to music

___Making jewelry

___Mechanics

___Miniature golf

___Painting

___Photography

___Playing cards

___Playing online games

___Praying

___Reading books

___Football

___Going online

___Going to a 12-Step meeting

___Going to church

___Going for a walk

___Hairstyling

___Ironing

___Journaling

___Knitting

___Making beats

___Martial arts

___Meditating

___Model railroading

___Part-time job

___Playing board games

___Playing instruments

___Playing video games

___Rapping

___Reading magazines

___Reading comics	___Running
___Scrapbooking	___Sewing
___Skateboarding	___Skiing
___Sleeping	___Snowboarding
___Soccer	___Spending time with pets
___Studying	___Surfing
___Surfing the web	___Swimming
___Taking showers or a bath	___Talking to friends
___Talking with a sponsor	___Tennis
___Texting	___Traveling
___Vacuuming	___Visiting relatives
___Volleyball	___Volunteer/community service
___Walking	___Walking the dog
___Watching movies	___Watching sports
___Watching television	___Weight-lifting
___Window shopping	___Woodworking
___Working the 12 Steps	___Wrestling
___Writing poetry	___Yearbook
___Yoga	___Youth ministry

Group Exercise and Discussion Topics for Self-Care

GROUP DISCUSSION

Self-care can take three forms—physical (the body); psychological (the mind); and emotional (the feelings)—all of which may be neglected when we are using substances. Likewise, recovery involves caring for ourselves in these ways. Explore how we may care for ourselves physically, psychologically, and emotionally. Is recovery really possible if we don't take care of ourselves in all three ways? Discuss.

GROUP DISCUSSION

Sleep is necessary for survival. Sleep allows the body to rest and rejuvenate, and allows the brain to process everything it "takes in" during the day. Thus, sleep is a form of self-care. Explore how sleep has been affected by substance abuse. How has the recovery process affected sleep patterns? Do group members have more difficulty falling asleep or staying asleep now? How has sleep been affected by the recovery process?

GROUP DISCUSSION

Days often begin or end with self-care practices. Discuss how individuals begin and end each day to maintain a balanced and healthy lifestyle. Discuss how failing to engage in self-care behaviors may be a warning sign of relapse.

GROUP DISCUSSION

Discuss the extrovert/introvert continuum. Where do group members fall individually, and what are some of the things we do as extroverts (e.g., social gatherings, group sports) or as introverts (e.g., reading, meditating)? Explore the advantages and disadvantages of being extroverted and being introverted. How does it affect recovery?

GROUP EXERCISE: TAKE-CARE BAGS

The materials needed for this exercise are lunch bags, index cards, pens, and art supplies. Give everyone in the group a bag to decorate as they wish. Give everyone a dozen index cards on which to write one activity they can do to relieve stress and take care of themselves (e.g., play basketball, go for a walk, listen to music, meditate). On the other side of each card, have them write an affirmation of encouragement to themselves (e.g., "I am a strong and confident person," "I won't let my stress control me or my life," "I can be free from alcohol and drugs"). When either stress or drug use is triggered, they can pull out one or more of the index cards and complete the activity on the card, one by one, until the stress is reduced significantly or it has passed.

Mindfulness

Mindfulness is attention and awareness to your present state. This requires using the senses to focus on the here-and-now, without thinking about the past or the future, and without making any kind of judgment (good or bad, right or wrong) of your own experience. Mindfulness benefits physical and emotional health and overall well-being. There are many health benefits to practicing mindfulness. It can reduce anxiety and lower heart rate, blood pressure, and pulse. It can increase immune system functioning and induce an overall state of calmness. Focusing your undivided attention on the present without judgment or interpretation also relaxes the mind, can stop or reduce worries, and may aid in relapse prevention. Mindfulness is a tool you can use to combat or manage cravings and urges to use, ease anxiety, and even aid in detoxification or withdrawal. By focusing on the present, you can reduce obsessive thoughts that trigger compulsive behaviors like drinking and drug use.

The following exercises in mindfulness may be done individually or in a group. You may choose to do one or both exercises. Also, you may choose to read these by yourself, or have someone like a group leader guide you through the exercises. Afterward, reflect on your experience(s) in the questions asked.

Exercise: Chair Exercise

Find a quiet comfortable place inside.

Sit down in a chair where you are comfortable and undisturbed.

Close your eyes.

Plant your feet on the floor.

Take slow deep breaths. [pause]

Clear your mind of all your worries, concerns, fears, and thoughts. [pause]

Focus your attention and awareness on your present surroundings only.

Pay attention to where you are in space. Are you in a room by yourself or with other people? Are you in a confined space or a large room indoors? [pause]

Focus on the physical sensations your body experiences. [pause]

Notice what you hear. [pause]

Do you hear noises like the ticking of a clock or soft music?

Notice if there are any odors or scents in the room.

Do you notice the scent of perfumes, household products, or air fresheners? [pause]

Notice the temperature in the room. Is it warm or cold? Is there a draft or breeze? Is there a fan, air conditioner, or heater on? [pause]

Remember to keep breathing deeply in and out. [pause]

Now focus your attention inward. [pause for a few minutes]

Take notice of what you are sitting on. Is it something hard like a wooden chair, or soft like a pillow or cushion? [pause]

Notice the texture of what you are sitting on, and the feel of the material against your back and on your behind. [pause]

Notice if you are sitting on something high or low to the ground, and if it is large or small. [pause]

Notice if the chair has arms, and if so, whether your arms are resting on the chair's arms. Are your arms extended? Or are your arms and hands folded on your lap? Notice the sensations in your arms and let go of any tension. [pause]

Now just sit there in quiet peace and focus on your present experience, your present sensations. Remember to keep breathing in and out, in and out. [pause]

Do not make any judgments or evaluations of what you experience. Just experience it. [pause]

Continue to just focus on the here-and-now for several minutes. When you are ready, open your eyes.

EXERCISE: Evaluate your experience in the following questions:

1. Mindfulness requires paying attention to the senses. What did you notice as you participated in the mindfulness exercise? What did you feel, hear, smell, and touch?

_____

_____

_____

2. What physical sensations did you notice in your body? Aches and pains? Tightness, tension, nervousness? Rapid or slow heart beat?

_____

_____

_____

Did these sensations decrease or go away by the end of the exercise?

_____

3. Did any thoughts enter your mind? If so, what were they and what did you do? Did you focus on the thoughts or erase them from your mind?

_____

_____

_____

Were the thoughts judgmental or evaluative in any way? Did you think at any point in the exercise that your experiences were good or bad, right or wrong, valuable or stupid, interesting or boring?

_____

_____

_____

4. How did you feel before the exercise vs. after the exercise? Did you feel calmer or less anxious? Tired or re-energized?

_____

_____

_____

EXERCISE: OUTDOOR MINDFULNESS

Find a quiet, comfortable place outside.

You may be outside in the yard, at a park, or in nature somewhere.

Sit or lie down and close your eyes.

Make sure you are comfortable.

Now focus on your breaths for a moment.

Take long deep breaths. As you breathe in the fresh air, imagine the air entering your mouth, traveling down your throat and into your lungs. Imagine your diaphragm filling up with oxygen. The air reaches every cell in your body, giving them all new energy.

Hold that breath. Then release it. Exhale. [pause]

Continue to breathe in and out, slowly. Take your time. Don't rush. [pause]

Notice the position of your body. Are you sitting on the ground or in a chair? Or are you lying down? Are your legs stretched or crossed? [pause]

Take notice if you are sitting on something hard like a wooden chair, soft like a blanket, or prickly like grass. [pause]

Are you alone outside? Are there people nearby? Are there animals near you? Flora and fauna? Tall trees? A body of water like a lake, a creek, or the ocean? Or a man-made swimming pool? [Pause for a few minutes, and remember to breathe.]

Take notice of the temperature. Is it a warm day? Can you feel the sun's rays shining down on you? Is there a gentle breeze or a gust of wind? [pause]

Notice what you hear. [pause]

Do you hear loud noises in the background, like a lawn mower or a car's engine? Are people talking in the distance? If you are near water, do you hear waves crashing or people splashing?

Do you hear soft noises like birds chirping, the babble of a brook, or leaves rustling? Maybe you hear a gentle wind blowing through the trees or the sounds of animals running around. [pause]

Notice any scents or odors. [pause]

Do you detect the faint scent of flowers, the freshness of the air, or the light scent of nature's fauna?

Continue to focus just on the present for several minutes. Remember to keep breathing deeply, in and out.

Now focus your attention inward. Remember to keep breathing in and out.

Imagine all your worries [pause], concerns [pause], judgments [pause], and thoughts [pause] just disappear.

Notice any body sensations like tension [pause], muscle tightness [pause], pain [pause], pressure [pause], or nervousness [pause].

Notice if your heart is beating fast or slow. Can you hear your own heart beating?

Now, imagine all these discomforts. Locate them in your body, beginning with your head, and move on down.

Imagine the tension, the tightness, the pain and pressure, and the anxiety just gathering like a wave as you move down your body. [pause]

Begin with your head [pause]. The wave then moves down into your face [pause], down your neck [pause], to your shoulders [pause], down your upper arms, down your elbows and lower arms [pause], down your hands and fingers [pause], and out your finger tips. [pause]. That wave of tension, stress, pain, and pressure flows out of your fingers. Flowing out slowly [pause for a few minutes].

Now imagine another wave of tension, pressure, and pain gathering in your chest, from your heart, lungs, diaphragm, stomach, kidneys, and all your vital organs. The wave is gathering and moving down your torso [pause].

Imagine any tension or pain that you hold in your back gathering into this wave as it moves downward, bringing relief and lightness to your body [pause].

The wave travels down your pelvis and buttocks [pause], moving into your hips [pause], down your groin [pause], and down your upper legs [pause]. The wave of tension, aches, and pains moves down your knees [pause], down your shins and lower legs [pause], into your ankles and feet [pause], and finally, out your toes [pause]. It is all flowing out your toes, bringing you relief and comfort.

All of the negativity is just flowing out of your body.

There is no more tension, tightness, pressure, or pain anywhere in your body as it all just flows out, bringing relief and relaxation.

At the same time, the warmth of the sun's rays is filling your body.

The negativity is flowing out of you as warmth and comfort is filling you. [pause for several minutes]

Remember to continue breathing deeply. [pause]

Continue to imagine your body releasing all the tension and filling up with warmth and light from the sun. Sit in this peace and calm for several minutes.

Pause for several minutes . . . After several minutes, focus your attention once again on your body and where you are in space. [pause]

Focus once again on your breathing. Breathe slowly in and out.

Slowly return to your own body.

Slowly count down from five [pause], four [pause], three [pause], two [pause], and one [pause]—

Slowly, and only when you feel ready, open your eyes. Adjust your eyes, as the brightness may hurt them. Do this over the course of a few minutes.

When you are done, reflect on your experience by answering the following questions, either by yourself or in the group:

1. Mindfulness requires paying attention to the senses. What did you notice as you participated in the mindfulness exercise? What did you feel, hear, smell, and touch?

_____

_____

_____

_____

2. What physical sensations did you notice in your body? Aches and pains? Tightness, tension, nervousness? Rapid or slow heart beat?

_____

_____

_____

_____

Did these sensations decrease or go away by the end of the exercise?

_____

3. Did any thoughts enter your mind? If so, what were they and what did you do? Did you focus on the thoughts or erase them from your mind?

_____

_____

_____

_____

Were the thoughts judgmental or evaluative in any way? Did you think at any point in the exercise that your experiences were good or bad, right or wrong, valuable or stupid, interesting or boring?

_____

_____

_____

4. How did you feel before the exercise vs. after the exercise? Did you feel calmer or less anxious? Tired or re-energized?

_____

_____

_____

_____

Group Exercise and Discussion Topics for Mindfulness

GROUP EXERCISE AND DISCUSSION

Have each individual in the group rate the following on a scale of 1 to 10 before completing the exercise on mindfulness:

- Depression (1 = not depressed at all; 10 = worst depression ever)

- Anxiety (1 = not anxious at all; 10 = worst anxiety ever)

- Anger (1 = not angry at all; 10 = most angry ever)

- Optimism/Pessimism (1 = very optimistic; 10 = very pessimistic)

- Positive/Negative attitude (1 = positive attitude; 10 = negative attitude)

- Hopefulness (1 = very hopeful; 10 = hopeless)

Following the exercise on mindfulness, have each group member rate each of these again, using the same scale of 1 to 10. Discuss where individuals fell before and after the exercise, noticing if scores decreased or increased at all. The lower the scores, the better the mood and attitude. Higher scores on depression, anxiety, and anger indicate more subjective depression, anger, and anxiety, while lower scores indicate less. The goal is to decrease scores using mindfulness. Higher scores on optimism/pessimism and positive/negative attitude indicate more subjective pessimism and negativity, while lower scores indicate more optimism and positivity. The goal, again, is to reduce ratings through the exercise. Discuss as a group.

> *Note:* Mindfulness can be a great coping skill
> to deal with urges to use and stress to prevent relapse.

GROUP DISCUSSION

Mindfulness can be challenging for some individuals because it requires an open mind, a willingness to focus on the present without dwelling on the past or future-tripping, and a willingness to suspend judgment or criticism. Discuss group members' experiences of the mindfulness exercise. Was it difficult or easy to be open-minded? Was it challenging to focus only on the here-and-now? Was it difficult to be nonjudgmental and uncritical? What made it easier?

Hope and Optimism

The road to recovery is usually a long and difficult journey with setbacks. It is important to maintain hope and optimism (looking toward the future with a positive attitude). This may be difficult at times. When we feel hopeless and pessimistic (negative) about the future and we don't see that "light at the end of the tunnel," we may need to rely on someone else to hold that hope and optimism for us until we feel stronger. There truly is a light, but sometimes we just can't see it.

EXERCISE

Answer the following questions:

1. How has negative and pessimistic thinking affected your substance abuse/addiction?

_____

_____

_____

_____

2. How do you define hope? What do you look forward to in the future? Do you consider yourself hopeful and optimistic?

_____

_____

_____

_____

3. What are the advantages and disadvantages of having a positive and optimistic attitude? How has this affected your recovery process?

_____

_____

_____

_____

4. What helps you maintain hope and optimism?

_____

_____

_____

_____

Group Exercise and Discussion Topics for Hope and Optimism

GROUP EXERCISE: AUTOGRAPH BOOK

The materials for this exercise include construction paper, a hole punch, string or ribbon, pens, and scissors. Have group members cut out pieces of paper at least 4" x 6". The number of pieces of paper should be equal to at least the number of people in the group, although they may choose to cut additional pieces. Punch the pieces of paper twice and tie them with a string or ribbon to hold them like a book. Have individuals write an uplifting and positive message on each sheet, and decorate the pages as they wish. Comments may be as simple as "You can stay clean and sober," or may be more lengthy and personal. Comments should encourage individuals to stay clean and sober and give them a lift when things get tough. More sheets can be added for friends or family. When complete, have members read through their books individually. The group may want to process thoughts and feelings related to this exercise.

GROUP DISCUSSION

Negative thinking and drug use tend to go hand-in-hand. Drug use often increases as your thinking becomes more negative and pessimistic—which, in turn, further increases your drug use. On the other hand, the more optimistic and positive you are about recovery, the less likely you are to use. Of course, there are always exceptions. What do group members think about this, and how can their thinking affect their ability to stay clean and sober?

GROUP EXERCISE AND DISCUSSION: MOVIE

Have the group watch the movie *The Blind Side* (2009), a true story about a youth who overcomes adversity and becomes a pro-football player. Discuss the following:

- How are hope and optimism depicted in the movie? Which characters are hopeful and optimistic?

- What difficulties and obstacles did Michael Oher face in his youth? What about in becoming a pro-football player? How did he overcome these obstacles?

- Who supported Michael, and how?

- What is the take-home message of the movie?

- Any leftover thoughts or feelings?

Gratitude

Too often, people take what they have for granted and focus on what they don't have. We forget to appreciate the little things like compliments or simple acts of kindness, and we often take for granted or even expect the bigger things we need for survival—shelter, food, good health, a job. As individuals with substance abuse and addiction problems, it is often the case that we don't appreciate what we have until it's gone, or until we've lost it. And with addiction, we risk losing these altogether and permanently through our behaviors.

EXERCISE

Answer the following questions:

1. Think of a time when you were given something (e.g., gift, card). What was it? What was it for? How did it make you feel?

_____

_____

_____

2. Now think of a time you gave something to someone else or went out of your way to do something nice for someone (e.g., opened a door for someone, gave a gift). How did it make you feel?

_____

_____

_____

3. Think of a person(s) for whom you are thankful. Explain why. How has this person helped you in your recovery process?

_____

_____

_____

4. Is there an object, place, or activity for which you are grateful? Why? How has this helped you in the recovery process?

_____

_____

_____

Group Exercises and Discussion Topics for Gratitude

GROUP EXERCISE: GRATITUDE TREE

For this exercise, you will need scissors, green and brown paper, pen(s), and tape or glue. Have everyone trace six leaves on colored paper and cut them out. They can decorate their leaves using an assortment of materials: pens, crayons, paints, glitter, stickers, etc. A large tree trunk and branches should also be cut. Have everyone write down three things for which they are thankful in their lives (e.g., family, friends, school, car) and three things for which they are grateful in their recovery/treatment (e.g., being clean and sober, sober peers, specific groups, counselors). Put one item per leaf. They can make more leaves if desired. Have group members share those things for which they are thankful as they tape their gratitude leaves to the tree trunk and branches.

GROUP DISCUSSION

Have each person in the group share the following: Think of someone or something that has helped you in the recovery process—your treatment program, a group, your support network, NA/ AA, a counselor. What is/was it, and how did it help? Discuss.

GROUP DISCUSSION

Giving back to others is an important aspect of the 12 Steps and other programs. Have group members share their experiences of giving back to someone (e.g., a gift, a nice comment, a gesture). What did that do for that person and how did it make you feel? How does helping others also help you? How does it affect recovery? Discuss.

GROUP EXERCISE: THANK-YOU CARD

For this exercise, you will need colored paper, pens, and art supplies of your choice. This exercise is to be completed by everyone in the group. Go back to Question 3 in the exercise above or think of someone else in your life for which you are thankful. Make a thank-you card to give to that person. Design it with the materials at hand. Address it to the person you are thanking and explain why you are grateful for him or her, then follow up by actually giving the card to the person.

Appendix: Making a Weekly Schedule

Tips for Making a Weekly Schedule

Structure is important in preventing relapse, so every relapse prevention plan needs a structured schedule. It's in those periods of time when we have no structure that we tend to use substances, often out of boredom. Those times may be in the afternoons, on Friday nights, or on the weekends. Therefore, structured schedules should include all seven days and nights of the week. A template is included.

Remember to schedule in school, activities, meetings or groups, therapy, and free time! It may be helpful to schedule in extra activities during those times of the day when you are most vulnerable or likely to relapse (e.g., Friday nights, weekends, immediately after school). Some activities need to be fun (e.g., sports practice, working out, band practice), and some need to be recovery-based to focus on relapse prevention (e.g., individual and family therapy, NA/AA meetings, outpatient groups).

Here are some guidelines for making a weekly schedule:

- Color-code your activities and color in blocks of time (e.g., school in yellow and part-time job in purple), as it is easier to see that way.

- Write down your most important activities first and fill in the extra spaces with things like chores.

- Don't have blocks of time that are empty, because that leaves opportunities to use. Again, make sure you have activities like groups, individual therapy, family therapy, and meetings that address substance abuse, relapse prevention, and clinical issues.

- Remember, NA/AA meetings are held every day at any time! To look for meetings in your area, go online to *www.na.org* or *www.aa.org*.

- If you don't have a part-time job, schedule in time to look for a job until you find one. This is especially important during the summer when school is out and there is way too much time to use.

Weekly Schedule:

TIME	MONDAY	TUESDAY	WEDNESDAY	THURSDAY
6:00 am				
7:00 am				
8:00 am				
9:00 am				
10:00 am				
11:00 am				
12:00 pm				
1:00 pm				
2:00 pm				
3:00 pm				
4:00 pm				
5:00 pm				
6:00 pm				
7:00 pm				
8:00 pm				
9:00 pm				
10:00 pm				
11:00 pm				
12:00 am				

The Adolescent Relapse Prevention Planner

TIME	FRIDAY	SATURDAY	SUNDAY
6:00 am			
7:00 am			
8:00 am			
9:00 am			
10:00 am			
11:00 am			
12:00 pm			
1:00 pm			
2:00 pm			
3:00 pm			
4:00 pm			
5:00 pm			
6:00 pm			
7:00 pm			
8:00 pm			
9:00 pm			
10:00 pm			
11:00 pm			
12:00 am			

References

Alcohol and Drug Consultation, Assessment and Skills Program (ADCAS). (2011a). Alcohol 101: Physical effects of alcohol. Retrieved April 23, 2011, from *http://www.wwu.edu/chw/preventionandwellness/AOD-WebPDFs/PhysicalEffectsofAlcohol.pdf*.

—————. (2011b). Alcohol 101: Alcohol and the body. Retrieved April 23, 2011, from *http://www.wwu.edu/chw/preventionandwellness/AODWebPDFs/Alcohol&theBody.pdf*.

Alcoholics Anonymous (AA). (2001). *Alcoholics Anonymous* (4th ed.). New York City, New York: Alcoholics Anonymous World Services, Inc.

American Chemical Society. (2007). Marijuana smoke contains higher levels of certain toxins than tobacco smoke. *ScienceDaily*. Retrieved May 3, 2011, from *http://www.sciencedaily.com/releases/2007/12/071217110328.htm*.

American Psychiatric Association. (2000). *Diagnostic and Statistical Manual of Mental Disorders* (4th ed., text revision). Washington, DC: Author.

Children's Hospital of Philadelphia. (2009). Heavy marijuana use may damage developing brain in teens, young adults. *ScienceDaily*. Retrieved April 6, 2010, from *http://www.sciencedaily.com/releases/2009/02/090202175105.htm*.

Chudler, E. (2006). Neuroscience for kids: MDMA. Retrieved February 25, 2011, from *http://faculty.Washington.edu/chudler/mdma.html*.

Finley, J. and Lenz, B. (1999). *Chemical Dependence Treatment Homework Planner*. New York: John Wiley and Sons, Inc.

Foundation for a Drug-Free World. (2009). *The Truth About Drugs: Real People, Real Stories* [Documentary]. (Available from Foundation for a Drug-Free World, 1626 N. Wilcox Avenue, #1297, Los Angeles, CA. 90028).

Hughes, J. (Producer) and Deutch, R. (Director). (1995). *Some Kind of Wonderful* [Motion picture]. United States: Paramount Pictures.

JAMA and Archives Journals. (2007, June 5). Low doses of ecstasy associated with decline in verbal memory. *ScienceDaily*. Retrieved May 3, 2011, from *http://www.sciencedaily.com/releases/2007/06/070604164938. html*.

Johnson, B., Kosove, A., and Netter, G. (Producers) and Hancock, J. L. (Director). (2009). *The Blind Side* [Motion picture]. United States: Warner Brothers.

Konrad, C. (Producer), Keach, J. (Producer), and Mangold, J. (Director). (2005). *Walk the Line* [Motion picture]. United States: Fox 2000 Pictures.

Litt, J. (2009). Formication. *Psychology Today*. Retrieved April 23, 2011, from *http://www.psychologytoday. com/blog/odd-curious-and-rare/200911/formication*.

Molecular Psychiatry. (2008). Possible connection between marijuana abuse and stroke or heart attacks. *ScienceDaily*. Retrieved May 3, 2011, from *http://www.sciencedaily.com/releases/2008/05/080513054830.htm*.

National Institute on Drug Abuse (NIDA). (2010a). NIDA Infofacts: Hallucinogens-LSD, peyote, psilocybin, and PCP. Retrieved April 27, 2010, from *http://www.nida.nih.gov/infofacts/hallucinogens.html*.

—————. (2010b). NIDA research report series: Inhalant abuse. Retrieved May 13, 2011, from *http:// www.nida.nih.gov/PDF/RRinhalants.pdf*.

—————. (2010c). NIDA research report series: Marijuana abuse. Retrieved April 23, 2011, from *http:// www.nida.nih.gov/PDF/RRMarijuana.pdf*.

—————. (2011a). NIDA InfoFacts: Cocaine. Retrieved January 12, 2011, from *http://www.nida.nih.gov/ infofacts/cocaine.html*.

—————. (2011b). NIDA for teens: Stimulants. Retrieved January 21, 2011, from *http://teens.drugabuse. gov/facts/facts_stim1.php*.

—————. (2011c). Mind over matter: The brain's responses to opiates. Retrieved April 15, 2011, from *http://teens.drugabuse.gov/mom/pdf/english/opiates.pdf*.

—————. (2011d). NIDA InfoFacts: Club drugs (GHB, ketamine, and rohypnol). Retrieved April 15, 2011, from *http://www.drugabuse.gov/infofacts/clubdrugs.html*.

Radiological Society of North America (RSNA). (2006, November 28). Ecstasy can harm the brains of first-time users. *ScienceDaily*. Retrieved April 23, 2011, from *http://www.sciencedaily.com/ releases/2006/11/061128084458.htm*.

Roediger, H., Capaldi, E. D., Paris, S., and Polivy, J. (1991). *Psychology* (3rd ed.). New York: Harper Collins Publishers.

Rosch, P. (1983). Effects of stress on the cardiovascular system. *Physician and Patient*, 2 (11), 30–44.

————. (1989). Stress addiction: Causes, consequences, and cures. In Frederic Flach (Ed.), *Stress and Its Management* (6) (pp. 103–116). New York: W.W. Norton & Co.

Sacks, D. O. (Producer). (2006). *Thank You for Smoking* [Motion picture]. United States: Twentieth Century Fox.

Selye, H. (1946). The general adaptation syndrome and the disease of adaption. *Journal of Clinical Endocrinology* (6), 117–120.

Sher, K. (1997). Psychological characteristics of children of alcoholics. *Alcohol Health and Research World*, 21(3), 247–254.

Society for Neuroscience. (2010). Human study shows greater cognitive deficits in marijuana users who start young. *ScienceDaily*. Retrieved May 3, 2011, from *http://www.sciencedaily.com/ releases/2010/11/101116104202.htm*.

Topping, J. (Producer) and Thomas, B. (Director). (2000). *28 Days* [Motion picture]. United States: Columbia Pictures.

Yale University. (2007). Long-term marijuana smoking leads to respiratory complaints. *ScienceDaily*. Retrieved May 3, 2011, from *http://www.sciencedaily.com/releases/2007/02/070212184119.htm*.

About the Author

 JENNIFER BRUHA, Ph.D. was born and raised in the San Francisco Bay Area, the eldest of two daughters to Donald and Janis Bruha. She attended the University of California, Los Angeles, where she earned a bachelor's degree in Psychology, followed by a master's degree in Counseling Psychology and a Certificate in Chemical Dependency Counseling from Notre Dame de Namur University. She earned a second master's degree and Doctorate (Ph.D.) in Clinical Psychology from the Institute of Transpersonal Psychology. She has been working as a clinician since 2003 at Our Common Ground, an adolescent residential treatment facility in Redwood City, California, and at the East Palo Alto adult treatment facility since 2009. She designed the Drug Education and Relapse Prevention curriculum at both facilities and continues to facilitate both groups. Her clinical and research interests include addiction, eating disorders, and trauma. In 2010, she was awarded the Alice Kahn Ladas Research Award for her research in mindfulness and eating disorders from the United States Association of Body Psychotherapy. *The Adolescent Relapse Prevention Planner* is her first book.

18996018R00129

Made in the USA
Middletown, DE
29 March 2015